DIGITAL MEDIEVAL

Published by Xstorical Publications Media, 2013

www.xstorical.com

Copyright © Jeremy M. Silver

British Library Cataloguing-in-Publication Data
Silver, Jeremy M
Digital Medieval / by Jeremy M. Silver

Cover and jacket design: Amir Gelbard
This print paperback edition
ISBN 978-0-9926805-2-7

 **Xstorical** Publications Media

DIGITAL MEDIEVAL

THE FIRST TWENTY YEARS OF MUSIC
ON THE WEB
...AND THE NEXT TWENTY

JEREMY SILVER

DEDICATED TO THE MEMORY OF

CYRIL LESLIE SILVER

1922 - 2012

TABLE OF CONTENTS

Introduction

Music led the way in developing the commercial and social potential of the web more than any other field with the one possible exception of pornography. My experiences of building businesses and exploring technology have largely focused on music and so this is not a book about porn.

Music is the canary in the gold mine of the internet for several very good reasons. Its appeal is global, its product is easily turned into very small digital files that can be easily shared and the technologists who developed the internet also had a great passion for music.

During the first twenty years of the world wide web, the music industry struggled to adapt. It spent most of the first decade (1993-2003) with its head in the sand trying to deny what was happening and then going to court trying to sue its way through change. In the second decade, the industry hitched its wagon so completely to Apple and its iTunes online store as to make it the default digital sales outlet for music in the Western world for a very long period until around 2006 when the first streaming services started to offer another means of accessing music.

The loss leading sale of music set Apple on the path to having the largest market capitalization of any company in the world. During this period, Google, Amazon, Facebook and Apple (GAFA) perfected their business models rapidly and highly successfully by developing varying degrees of "walled gardens" where consumers could access content easily from within but, increasingly, could only consume inside the walls of the garden. The deal to the consumer is hardly made explicit. The offer looks great but the full price is never entirely clear. In fact many observers are still trying to work out exactly what that price is. It takes the form of either a free service offered in exchange for personal data that leads to significant losses of privacy (Google and Facebook) or great technological value and convenience at competitive prices where the devices and the content are tied increasingly tightly together (Apple and Amazon - you can only read your book on the Kindle platform or play your music on the iPhone, iPad or Macbook). Either way the business goal is to lock a consumer into one platform, one cloud-based solution and one set of devices. Success means the consumer's data and content is locked in and becomes very hard to transfer out. The walled gardens are decorative and beautiful until their walls get too high for comfort.

Music's mass appeal and global nature has played a key role in attracting consumers into the walled gardens of GAFA. Music companies have been willing to trade both product value and market influence for access to new digital internet markets, to which they were singularly unable to adapt their business models in any other way. So it was that music and later books, film and tv became the loss leaders to many more high margin products and services.

As they have grown, GAFA companies have sought to achieve increasing degrees of vertical integration and this is only set to continue. They want to secure consumers for whom their chosen brand becomes an all-embracing solution for the consumer's entire life-needs. In this context, major music labels may aspire to create some degree of interoperability between services, but they have little leverage against the internet giants who they helped build up throughout the first decade of the 21st century. The reality is that once inside the walled gardens of GAFA, consumers will see the walls begin to rise. My music is in the cloud, but soon enough my medical records will be in the cloud, my home security will be managed from the cloud, my banking and my energy needs too. If a consumer subscribes to one cloud service, then they are very likely to continue with all the extensions of that cloud service platform rather than mix and match. It becomes increasingly inconvenient to remain service agnostic. The dominant players nurture their "walled-gardens" of creative content and other services tethered to their digital formats and devices. As the competition for consumers increases, so does the need to make the walls higher, the content inside still more attractive and the data-lock-in even tighter. The "walled-gardens" gradually turn into virtual "digital cities". Today it is mostly content that is locked in but increasingly these companies will develop their online services. What works for content today, will work for medical health records tomorrow. While not being able to move my music from the Apple cloud to the Amazon cloud may be a minor inconvenience, not being able to move my medical records may be a matter of life or death. The entertainment industry has been a critical factor in the developing success of these major players. The GAFA companies now seem set to dominate entire the landscape not just the entertainment sector. How soon walled gardens will become digital city states is hard to forecast. Some say they have already become so. We may all already inhabit the digital medieval landscape.

Western consumers are dominated by Google, Amazon, Facebook, Apple. In the East, Ali Baba, Two Cent, Baidu and Weibo are similar giants. The competition between city-states is to the occasional short-term benefit of consumers but mostly it is at their long-term expense. The companies slug it out in market places, but also wage legal battles in court (Apple and Samsung most notably, recently). Occasionally they will form flimsy somewhat unexpected alliances such as the one between Microsoft and Facebook. These are often as much about trying to hold back the competition as they are about real collaboration. While internecine fights dominate the digital medieval landscape, we also see regular battles between digital city-states and nation states. Efforts to regulate the new global powers are hampered by local geography that is largely ignored on the Internet.

Digital medieval is not unlike the analogue medieval. The old rule of law has been abandoned and the moral compass of businesses begins to spin. The experience of the first dot-com bubble was often said to be akin to the pioneering days of the Wild West, but I think the medieval period provides us with a much more extensible analogy to where we find ourselves today.

In the digital medieval environment, everyone experiences a communal sense of rapid and vertiginous change which brings into question the shared world-view of the past. Digital medieval forces the abandonment of old truths before new realities have become fully formed. It creates corporate anxieties that prompt ill-considered acquisitions of companies at excessive valuations. It spawns soothsayers and internet gurus. It places young inexperienced executives in charge of social media marketing because they appear to understand these things better. The effect is to create a digital economic landscape where no one is sure of the rules and a few players dominate in a wilderness of many independent smallholdings.

Inside the content verticals, the major studios or publishing houses perform very similar roles, seeking to hoover up creators and consumers; consolidating increasingly as they fear the might of the city-states. Random House's recent acquisition of Penguin from Pearson was explicitly as a means to increase their scale and thus their leverage with Amazon, whilst not seeking to make sudden changes to their business model. In music, that means a few major labels signing fewer bands and many more bands seeking to make themselves heard by direct communication with their fans. In the technology world, this means the upsurge in startups and the pursuit of them by investors leading to the creation of dot-com bubbles.

Coexisting with the majors in their fortress states, scattered around and about, like so many digital serfs ("micro-serfs"), working on their online smallholdings, subsist the cottage-industry businesses of independent companies, startups, individual creators and all their respective brands. Whether they're bands or startups, some of these smallholdings will develop dependencies and supplicant relationships with the digital city states. Some remain resolutely independent and develop their own sustainable communities of customers. Some of them will seek to scale fast and aspire to become new city states themselves. The global growth of the "Maker Movement", fueled by the low cost hardware like Arduino and Raspberry Pi and the increasing availability of cheap 3D printers is also encouraging a global local interest in cottage industry production, of communities making things for themselves. Local community based genomic laboratories doing individual DNA research is another reflection of this organic growth at the grass-roots level.

No good medieval landscape is complete without its share of disruptive invaders. It is, of course, no coincidence that just below the surface of the digital medieval lurks the "digital media evil". It is represented by notorious disrupters such as the anti-heroes of Napster, the convicts of the Pirate Bay and the Baron Mega-Upload himself, Mr. Kim Dot Com. There are numerous more Anonymous unholy hoards offering in more or less plain-sight, free music downloads and video streams, providing digital locker services for sharing at the blurred fringes of legality, exploiting the geographical anomalies of the law, and attracting advertising spend from indiscriminate media-buying networks. The pirates and digital vandals remain the sworn enemies of the studios. Their "anti-piracy" crusades began in the early part of the period, and their huge commercial losses are laid squarely at the pirates' doors.

Between 1999 and 2013, the global recorded music industry lost more than half of its value. According to the International Federation of Phonographic Producers (IFPI), recorded music was worth, in 1999, over $35bn in global trade revenues. Today, that figure is just over $16bn. As it sought to transition from a physical disc-based business to a digital online one, it stumbled, misstepped and lashed out irrationally. Catastrophically, it responded by suing its customers on a mass scale. Through inflexible, opaque and increasingly archaic contracts, it ended up encouraging some of its most successful artists to abandon the record business and take up independent careers. On a very few occasions it took advantage of the dot-com bubble to great short-term economic benefit, but generally the industry has been consistent in using its trade associations to attack technology companies and lobby for increased regulation of the internet. It has carried on this anti-technology medieval crusade through its trade association representatives at the RIAA, IFPI and in the UK, the BPI, even as the commercial directors of the individual companies did everything they could to place the online and digital sales future of the industry into the hands of those same big GAFA companies.

The advent of the online era saw the slow slide of an entire industry into its own digital medieval period. The era of CD sales in the 80s and 90s had been the music industry's golden age of antiquity. Revenues were higher in this period than they had ever been before or would ever be again. The industry kept CD prices high, taking advantage of digital production processes to reduce manufacturing costs. But the digital genie was out of the bottle and moving into the hands of consumers. The internet brought about the virtual collapse of music's holy CD empire and revenues started to decline dramatically. Many believed that the internet would effectively destroy the music industry completely. They were wrong, but the time it took to transform itself and the twists and turns along the way of doing so have been tortuous to behold. One can only hope they might be instructive to others. The increasingly dark experiences of this one industry, anticipate the digital medieval that others are now in the midst of too. Indeed, I believe that we are all on the edge of something akin to a more broadly defined digital medieval period.

The fate of the music industry is well-understood as the first example of what is inevitable for all creative content industries as they are impacted by the internet. Less frequently discussed is the degree to which the entrepreneurial business model of music parallels that of technology start-ups. With the surge in entrepreneurship brought on by the worldwide web, the parallels increased. The entrepreneurial nature of the music industry also foreshadowed the responses to the internet of other kinds of large corporation and what online start-up culture looks like today. A&R people (music industry talent developers) and venture capitalists who find, filter and place informed bets on green-shoot opportunities have much in common

Today, despite its checkered past, the music industry is more optimistic about its digital future. The major labels are seeing growth in online digital revenues. While there is still a gap between declining physical and rising digital sales, it looks less life threatening than it once did. The industry has scaled back to accommodate it. The major labels have consolidated from five in the early 1990s (Sony, Warner, Polygram, EMI,

Bertelsman), to three today (Sony, Warner, Universal). Many independent labels have dropped by the wayside. Many new digitally focussed businesses have grown and evolved into a healthy new ecosystem that is becoming fit for purpose. Companies like Beggars Banquet, PIAS, Kobalt, InGrooves and Consolidated Independent have also demonstrated how retaining an independent ethic and investing in digital has made it possible to evolve with less pain and greater efficiency.

The surrounding eco-system of new service providers is still in a state of flux. The iTunes domination of music labels' digital revenues is beginning to be challenged by new services like Spotify and Deezer, as well as by the cloud-locker, music services of Google and Amazon.

Some of the more progressive content companies, like Universal Music and Pearson Publishing, have started to display the results of the root and branch reform which has been forced upon them. Inside these companies, the reality is acknowledged that so-called "piracy" on the internet is likely to persist just as counterfeiting exists in the physical world. While they still instruct their lobbyists to pursue the anti-piracy crusades, their commercial focus is increasingly on innovation and transformation. Some of them are starting to look more like truly digital businesses and are beginning to see the success of their lower cost-bases, and increased online sophistication. It has been a generational shift.

I was fortunate enough to be working in the turbulent heart of the music industry during this period of immense change. It precipitated a winding personal journey of my own. I went from geeky enthusiast to corporate gatekeeper, to passionate entrepreneur, adviser and blogger in ten years from 1993 to 2003. The addictiveness of connectivity, change and innovation has hardly waned throughout. This account of what happened in the first twenty years of music on the web, and what

I think may happen in the next twenty, is a doubtless deeply flawed exploration of some of the key events as they unfolded, a discussion of the big ideas that informed transformation and my personal record of some of the characters involved. It is an insider account of how a flashy, glamorous global business learned very slowly to change and adapt to new circumstances. It is also a reflection on the significant shifts in thinking provoked by the first major industry's online encounter with the twenty-first century.

Throughout this period, a culture clash between technology and creative content has been one of the defining characteristics on display. The glaring gaps and failures in communications between "the people, the poetry and the pipes" have continued. Ironically, many of the legislative efforts to overcome the problems between these sectors only served to intensify them. The same friction continues today at a corporate and infrastructural level. It continues to inhibit areas of innovation too, although there are encouraging signs of it diminishing and occasionally disappearing all together in start-ups and new "converged" businesses.

The transition of music to the digital economy is not yet complete, but it is more fully formed than in many other media sectors. Many of the experiences that music companies have undergone are relevant to other creative business sectors such as print publishing, film production, games development and television. The models may vary to some degree, but the disintermediation, the new entrants and the disruption of distribution are all consistent. The realities of digitization, compression and the internet make all creative content copyable, globally distributable and consumable as soon as it is released. The rapid growth in the popularity of ebooks is an example of how publishing has learned in part from music's failings. Yet, the story is far from over as publishing houses, distributors and retailers are reeling from the changes in the economics, fueled largely by Amazon's substantial strategic investment in its Kindle platform - tethering content to their proprietary devices. As for the film and television industries, they have been protected by the large file sizes of their output. But with increasingly available high-speed broadband (fixed and mobile), their transition to the digital economy is well overdue. The rapid escalation of these new realities will, I believe, lead eventually to significant changes in the regulatory environment, changes to copyright law, and changes to service offerings. For now though, traditional businesses remain resistant to any kind of fundamental reform because they are caught in a trap. The short term needs of their old business models always mitigate against the new ones. This phenomenon has been called Tarzan economics. Even as companies need need to move forward in the jungle, they have difficulty swinging from the old reliable business model's liana to a new and untested one. The demands of shareholder value and the stock market conspire to prioritize today's bottom line against tomorrow's innovation strategy.

The web's level playing field allows any new business to test its ideas with a community of live consumers. As many have observed, it is quite simply the most powerful enabler of change since the industrial revolution, the most amazing global research lab. This very openness is the basis upon which the digital medieval landscape could eventually burst into the flowering of a digital renaissance. As start-up fever spread into the technology sector through the liberating effects of the internet and the web, a tension has increasingly become apparent between "openness" and proprietary approaches to the market.

The web and the mp3 appeared on the market in the same year as each other, 1993. It was not just show business paranoia that made it appear that these technologies were conspiring to undermine the industry. Both the web and the mp3 are massively successful examples of how open software and infrastructure can stimulate innovation and enable new business models. The immediate response of the major corporates to the openness of the web was to try to tie down and secure music's passage through it. Equally, they tried to create controllable proprietary standards for the net's architecture and for audio compression in the face of mp3's increasing popularity.

Impassioned, individualistic, entrepreneurship became the most rapid means of exploring the web's potential. At the same time though, the studios displayed surprisingly emotional, almost visceral reactions to the loss of their business model. Considering the ultra-rational business mentality of these corporations, their response to such dramatic change maps surprisingly accurately onto human responses to grief. As this narrative moves back and forth between the specifics of behavior inside the music industry and broader economic and social shifts, the parallels are frequently very close. Music is a youth cultural phenomenon as well as an industry. In its broadest sense, music has been amenable to digitization and led the way. It opened up thinking about the social, cultural and economic impact of moving not just individual businesses, but entire industrial sectors and indeed much of our lives, onto the internet.

With the growth of mobile devices and the mobile web, the battle between open and proprietary consumer offerings has accelerated still further. Apps and app stores represent a greater lock-in than simple websites ever did. The walled gardens, which began as simply the preserve of content are extending to other kinds of services, from the digitized playlist to the quantified self of the "Fitbit", or the Nike "fuel band" or the

Jawbone "Upband". The GAFA digital city states are raising their ramparts to lock consumers more firmly inside. In the coming twenty years, a further wave of digital medievalism may well embrace us.

Digital city-states will begin to rival actual nation states. Treaties and understandings will be signed between them. On February 1st 2013, the International Herald Tribune displayed on its first screen, a photograph of the French President, Francois Hollande sitting down with Eric Schmidt, CEO of Google Inc to sign a multi-million Euro trade deal with a group of prominent French publishers. This is not the first instance of a digital city-state making a publicly signed agreement with an actual nation state, but it may be the first time that the leaders have been photographed together as if they were both "heads of state". Treaties and trade agreements are fundamentally designed to avoid legal and military battles. Digital medievalism is also characterized by massive increases in legal and cyber warfare conducted between nation states and digital city-states. Patent wars and malware wars are already in the common armory of these factions, with content often used as the vehicle for transmission. Cyber warfare currently may only have delaying or interruptive effects, but in the near future, human lives will become vulnerable as collateral in a more digitized world. The US and Europe are already on a fast track to digitize their medical care services, incorporating interfaces and user experiences learned by developers in the games, TV and music industries. The web and digital technologies are enabling connected, remote patient monitoring, tele-diagnosis and record keeping. As this virtualization of care accelerates and extends to every dimension of our lives from health to finance to transport to energy, the risks from cyber disruption extend to human life itself.

At the very heart of all this debate is the data that every transaction and interaction throws up. Big data has become a buzzword of industry in the last few years, and it sits at the heart of what some perceive of as the consumer entrapment that characterizes the digital medieval experience. There are of course all kinds of big data; public, private, transactional, logistical, user-generated, linked, open, transient, real-time and so on. But the access to individual private data, the very fumes of the internet's acceleration and how we negotiate the complex relationships around it place global societies and economies at a crossroads. The recent controversies surrounding Streetview and Prism are just the tip of the iceberg. What we think of Google's "inadvertent" gathering of consumer data in its Streetview project or how we position the US National Security Service's Prism surveillance reach as revealed by Wikileaks activist and political refugee, Edward Snowden, will determine how future governments and companies respond to the data challenge and opportunity. The challenges these kinds of activities represent are global. They occur beyond the reach of individual governments or nation states. At the same time, there are currently very few global institutions sufficiently technologically literate to regulate these kinds of behaviors let alone combat the more direct cyber-military threats. Perhaps we need to be thinking about creating some new, well-governed, global public institutions to help us cope with these emerging global realities.

Music and creative content companies have struggled through the advent of the web as if it were the dark ages, rife with anarchy and conflict for the last twenty years. As we enter the second twenty years of the web, will music and the rest of the creative industries descend further into dark and medieval conditions or will they rise up from their trauma into a long awaited digital renaissance? The choices that governments, companies and consumers make in the next twenty years of the web will precipitate Western economies along a road which may take them rapidly toward a true digital renaissance of innovation and growth or plunge them deeper into darker more sinister digital medieval times. The choice is ours.

1. Connected addicted

We've all become junkies of the internet. We feel anxious if we're disconnected. We can't wait to download a new app, a new song, a new tweet from a friend. If we don't connect or check our feed, we feel we're missing out, nobody loves us, we've become less significant, less validated as human beings than we were. This delusion has become a normality. At first it was subversive behaviour among a few cogniscenti, now it is possible that all of humanity is evolving before our eyes to adopt versions of these behaviours. The constant reference to our devices for digital self-affirmation is as natural as breathing. We take our devices with us everywhere, to bed, to the bathroom. We strap them to our bodies when we go running or to the gym, we plug them into our ears on planes. Google is rolling out its augmented reality online Glass and the thought of having chips or other forms of prosthesis implanted to enhance our performance or our capabilities seems less distant than it was. Becoming cyborgs seems an inevitability.

In the autumn of 1993, I sat at my desk in the bedroom of my flat in West Hampstead, London and peered into the screen of my Apple Powerbook, looking at the future. By today's standards, the machine was bulky and clunky, made of thick grey plastic with a large roller-ball for a mouse. This was the first model of laptop Apple ever produced and I had just smuggled it in from the US. Plugged into the Powerbook was a tiny spherical camera housed in a pyramid stand that allowed it to rotate like a chameleon's eye. Cameras like this are built into consumer electronics devices all the time now, but in the early nineties this was extraordinary technology even if it did only manage a low res, black and white image. A colour camera would take another two years to come out. On the screen, CUCMe (pronounced see you see me) software produced large blocks of square pixels which gradually resolved into a series of screen images. It was a mind-blowing breakthrough for the intellectual minority who populated this weird live network. Most of the participants were academics in places like Stanford, University of Minnesota, and MIT, staring at each other, waving, smiling or looking distractedly in the wrong direction. One night, I noticed I was getting quite a lot of attention and couldn't work out why. Then I realised with amusement and embarrassment that my girlfriend was getting ready for bed and could be seen, over my shoulder, taking off her clothes. For a moment, I was inadvertently, the publisher of a global soft porn channel. No wonder these guys kept coming back to check out CUCMe.

There is a reason drug addicts call their dealers their connection. Web surfers have become familiar with the addictive power of immersive environments. The anonymity of the web and the randomness of the connections made are big factors. The environments may be as varied as the animated virtual Second Life (launched in 2003) or the curiously compulsive video connection of Chatroulette which flowered briefly in 2009. At first, the compulsion was simply the amazing feat of connection. It was great fun to go into these audio and video environments and connect with random people all over the world and wave at one another. Predictably enough, basic human urges had much to do with this and as CUCMe gained in popularity so did the number of men who chose to put their cameras under their desks and between their legs, to wave to the world. Things became more sophisticated pretty fast of course. At its peak, Second Life, was taken over by hundreds of users who turned their avatars into winged penises and flew around the virtual world in strangely beautiful flocks. Chatroulette deteriorated almost immediately into a random sea of waving male members. In many respects, the history of the web has been populated by a bunch of pricks in flight, looking to penetrate new markets or spearhead the next big thing. Pornographers were often the innovators online, not just in the use of webcams, but also in the development of transaction engines, sales, marketing and subscription schemes.

In the early days, the very difficulty of getting on line was part of what made the web an addictive cult. Connecting to the internet involved a complicated and patchy procedure. The 24,000 baud modem plugged into the phone line and dialled into switches, and then made a sequence of nasty hissing and sucking noises, a kind of digital copulation. When it finallly connected, it fell silent, probably smoking some kind of digital cigarette in a roseate afterglow in some telephone exchange somewhere in Hampstead. Technology improves rapidly so we quickly moved up to 56k modems but speeds were still painfully slow and connections were erratic. Connecting had a slightly illicit feeling. It seemed as if we were trying to make the technology do things that it wasn't intended should be done along phone lines. Fledgling internet service providers were popping up and offering connectivity. Demon Internet was the earliest in the UK. Their name picked up on the underground, counter-cultural excitement of the experience. Earthlink in the US had more of a cyber-hippy vibe.

In 1991, a couple of years before the advent of the web, I joined Virgin Records as Head of Press. The company had just been acquired by the EMI Group for $1bn. Its established acts included the Rolling Stones, Genesis, Phil Collins, Meat Loaf, Janet Jackson, and Lenny Kravitz. These were supplemented by a diverse range of new stars like Massive Attack, the Verve, the Smashing Pumpkins and the Spice Girls. The company was based on a campus spanning the Union Canal, off London's Ladbroke Grove. Artists, managers and record company executives mingled in the party atmosphere of this highly social setting. The art of doing business here was a sophisticated mix of laid-back and cut-throat. In these halcyon times, early addicts like me, found it challenging to get anyone in music to understand the Internet. I initially persuaded Virgin to get online because it offered a whole new means of gaining publicity for artists. The record industry was experiencing its greatest boom of all time and, unbeknown to its shareholders, it was also enjoying its final period of growth in profitability. The nineties were the pay-out years when the investment in CDs brought huge profits as music fans re-purchased much of the music they already owned on vinyl. As multi-media CD-ROMs arrived, executives looked on them as new formats out of which they could make a further killing. Inasmuch as they were aware of it, the internet didn't seem so different. If music fans could get addicted to it, then record labels could probably make money out of it - eventually.

In 1993, no worldwide web existed; no web browser to help us navigate, no web to navigate. Instead, there were directories of files on computers dotted around the world which could be accessed by a File Transfer Protocol (FTP) program. Many early adopters used a Mac client called Fetch. It featured an animated cartoon terrier running eagerly across the screen, perpetually and enthusiastically chasing down that virtual bone. What he actually brought back was listings of the contents of university libraries. Quite a stretch in the imagination seemed needed to go from these dry offerings to a new entertainment medium. Other programmes proliferated, the University of Minnesota produced a programme called Gopher - named after the university's mascot. It subsequently enjoyed an upgrade and became TurboGopher. Using these programmes to look at the content of the University of Minnesota library from my bedroom in West Hampstead seemed pretty cool. To download the text of an actual abstract was mind blowing. Only a few of these FTP sites existed. You had to know the addresses before you could go there. I used to find out the interesting new FTP sites from Wired magazine, the new bible of the internet, first published in January 1993 and only available in the UK, in a famous alternative bookshop, called Compedium in London's Camden Town. Compedium sewed the counter-cultural seed that spawned today's sprawling Camden street market, the largest hipster bazaar in Europe. Back then, it gave us a connection with California, which seemed to be inventing a new future on a monthly basis - and Wired was the bong of the internet.

The alternative culture of post-hippy, post-punk anti-corporate "empowerment of the people" fed right into this accelerating cycle of technology innovation. The power of global communication becoming accessible in our bedrooms felt subversive from the start. While browsing for academic papers, it became obvious in 1993 that people were also posting other stuff, like music. As I fetched and gophered around these ftp sites, I found clips by people like Brian Eno, Tangerine Dream and the Future Sound of London. At first the clips only lasted ten seconds. They could have been longer, even thirty seconds if it weren't for the glacial speed of file transfer. The kind of music being posted was the indicator of the way in which alternative culture and technological innovation were going hand in hand. This development of the internet, despite its military forebears, had all the trappings of community activism. I presented the internet to fellow Heads of Department at Virgin. I showed them an FTP site on the other side of the planet and the clips of music by our bands. I told them this was going to change their world. They were curious for a moment, amazed at the technology and then increasingly indignant that "their music" could be up there.

When they realised I was serious, they laughed uncontrollably. They told me I'd been staying up way too late again. They were right about that. I couldn't find enough hours in the day to accommodate the fascination for what was unfolding. The addiction was perceptible in the red-rimmed eyes of early surfers.

When it did arrive, the web would be a little easier on our eyes but no much less addictive than crack. It did not arrive with a great fanfare, but with a groan and a stumble. The original Mosaic programme was created at the US National Super Computing Centre, a research institute at the University of Illinois. Its name hinted at its patchwork nature, drawing together different components of text and graphics to make a whole display. It fell over a lot and when it did stay up, there wasn't that much to see. Tim Berners Lee, a British nuclear research scientist, had created the concept of the world wide web and the hyper-text markup language that enabled it a few years earlier, during his time at the CERN research centre in Switzerland (better known for its work on the Large Hadron Collider and the search for the Higgs Boson, the so-called God Particle, a key element in quantum physics). The internet had emerged out of the US military's desire to create a communications network that would be resistant to nuclear attack and always be able to route around an area that had been knocked out. Berners Lee created the means to navigate it and the new browser rendered it graphical. Now the early addicts had more than file-names and directory structures with which to surf.

Netscape emerged in November 1994 as a more professionally produced product that set the standard for the next few years. The Netscape company was led by Marc Andreessen an internet pioneer and Jim Clarke, the founder of Silicon Graphics. Both went on to become leading Silicon Valley investors. The name Netscape with its perky logo of an animated letter N stepping over the edge of a planet, suggested the global impact of the new technology, but it still managed to feel underground and alternative.

This technology-driven edginess fitted right in with the culture of electronica bands like Daft Punk, the Future Sound of London, Massive Attack and Fluke who all happened to be signed to Virgin labels in the early nineties. Building a website to promote them seemed like the obvious response to all the technology coming out of California. Musician and writer David Toop introduced me to net-head Paul Sanders. Sanders ran a music production company in the old Truman's Brewery in Brick Lane. The neighbourhood wasn't trendy then, just cheap, roomy and damp. He and his friends were ex-Cambridge boffins with an ear for music and a nose for the future. I hired them to help create the website. We approached it with high ideals. We did not want it to have any Virgin branding - let alone a hint of corporate EMI. The site was only going to feature a select group of artists who fitted the rave and indie web vibe. This would be one of the first music driven websites in the world and the only one of its kind in Europe. It was an insider medium for a small group who liked to think they were ahead of the curve. Turns out this time they were.

The complexity of having to dial in, sometimes connecting, sometimes not, gave the internet its mystery. Science fiction writer William Gibson had already coined the term cyberpunk in his debut novel Neuromancer (1984). His work fed our imaginations about what the web could be capable of achieving and with the influence of Wired's alternative outlook, with some amusement, we started to see ourselves as cyberpunks. The Matrix movie of 1999 contributed to this romanticising of the same cyber counter-culture. We were "jacking" in all the time and if we were not online then we were either frustratedly looking to jack in or impatiently waiting until we next could.

We called the website, The Raft, a name that came from Neal Stephenson's novel SnowCrash, which depicted a seminal vision of a virtual world. The raft in his book is populated by roving pirates who lurk offshore and create havoc, hacking into communications systems, distributing subversive messages like pirate radio broadcasters. Off-shore, pirate culture from music web 1.0, has continued to Pirate Bay and Mega-upload. The robber barons of a new medievalism will continue to be the visible tip of a dark net which grows, mostly invisible at a faster pace than the mainstream internet and with much more sinister intent. In the niche naïveté of Web 1.0, the simplest communication networks were cool, where anyone could share files and chat, artists could build relationships with listeners who actually talked back.

While Virgin culture celebrated the weird, the music industry was in denial - the internet was clearly never going to be the mainstream. Virgin's UK Managing Director, Paul Conroy, had hired me because I was not the typical music industry type. He would occasionally accuse me of looking pale and staying up too late, but he was a talent spotter by nature and let us keep working on The Raft and involve some other people. To start with there was nothing, no computers, not even an internet connection at Virgin's office. We couldn't launch a website on a painfully slow, 24,000 baud modem. So we went on an entrepreneurial offensive.

We persuaded Sun Microsystems to sponsor us with kit and publicity. Sun manufactured the hardcore servers on which websites run. For them, the judicious handing out of free computers to emergent web developers made good marketing sense. We felt like we were being a touch subversive, sewing some seeds which might just have a disruptive impact on the conventional music industry. At the same time we were taking advantage of the popularity of music to saunter into a large corporate office in the city and persuade them to give us free equipment. We got a Sparc 5 box and a fancy Voyager Unix luggable computer that looked as if was designed to manage a space mission. Our marketing contact at Sun, Louise Proddow had a wild, dyed-blond enthusiasm for the web. She was much happier doing business with some guys from a record label than with her usual corporate IT purchasers. We didn't even have to put their logo on the website.

Our next task was to get Virgin Records better connected than through the old twisted copper pair of the telephone line. Imperial College (whose Computer Department was already leading the UK) lies about two miles south east of the Virgin campus. We discussed our project with them. It was an easy negotiation. On hearing our plans, they said we were clearly planning large scale research into students, the internet and music. We agreed with that description. They said that if we could find someone to make a physical connection (ie lay some cable or a pipe), they would connect us to SuperJanet - the Superfast Joint Academic Network that linked to the very backbone of the internet. Andrew Curry of Videotron, the Canadian company who owned the West London cable franchise, agreed that he needed to give Virgin a high speed T1 line into its offices because world famous bands would use his cable network thus bestowing fame, fortune and fairy dust on all associated with them. Curry is now one of the UK's leading futurists based at the Henley Management Centre. While most people were feeling hot if they had a 56k modem, we were streaming music from some of the best bands in the world at terabytes-a-second. This small piece of the early development of the web already contained the heady mix of addiction and entrepreneurialism which has gone on to define it.

The Raft launched in the autumn of 1994 at almost exactly the same time as the first version of the Netscape browser. It coincided with Virgin's annual International Conference. We set up a massive screen in the boardroom and talked the hundred or so delegates through the site and got excited cheers from our colleagues from 60 countries around the world. We did the interviews with the Guardian, the BBC and Channel 4 news who were all getting excited about digital innovation. It was all in the name of great promotion for the bands and we achieved high profile publicity for a lot less than it would cost to make a video. As the web grew, the appetite for new functionality grew with it. Shockwave from Macromedia, which eventually turned into Flash from Adobe started to offer so-called "rich media" experiences inside webpages. While initially, we only had 30 second clips of music and a few cool animated graphics, before long we were running webcasts, video streams and inviting artists to join online chats with their fans. In a series of editorial features, we would ask artists to come in and empty their pockets. We scanned the contents (always seemed to include packets of Rizla cigarette rolling papers and bits of cardboard). We uploaded everything we could to the website. We created a new kind of bond between the personal lives of the bands and their fans. We got as addicted to telling stories on the web as we were to finding new ways to play with the technology.

The other thing this addiction produced was data - tons of it. The theory of big data and how our world is waiting to be informed by it, is well known. Highly sophisticated techniques are being worked on all the time to track and analyse consumer traffic across the web. When we launched The Raft, the only thing we had were raw data logs generated by servers. The site attracted visitors from all over the globe, so we wanted to know how people found the site, which pages were most popular which were the least visited, and which countries visitors were from. We wanted to be able to tell our international marketing folk which countries which artists were popular in on the internet. At first we got some basic data which we duly circulated, but we wanted to get a sense of it in real time. I set our IT team onto trying to come up with a statistical analysis programme that could follow users through the sites, visualise their movements in real time. We had a notion that we could have web jockeys who could change the content of pages according to what was popular or "trending" and do deals with other sites as we learned where people came from and where they went after they left us. It took the IT team a year to figure out that they didn't have a machine big enough to process all the data that the website produced. They also realised that they had nothing powerful enough to begin to process all the data even if they could progressively store it. We were seeing the beginnings of Big Data and the potential for online marketing on which companies like Google and Facebook have subsequently built their empires. It was a decade before a company like Semetric with its entertainment industry-wide focus on big data and its Musicmetric product would be capable of beginning to attack this scale of problem and handle the even larger quantities of data hauled off today's web.

The internet just got more and more addictive. Wifi would not arrive for another six years (early 2001), so until then we were constantly meddling with handsets and disconnecting phone lines in hotel bedrooms. "Phone phreaking" began hacker culture, simply centred on finding ways to make free long distance calls from public phone boxes. As a tribute, 2600, the hacker magazine, still featured on its back cover until recently, celebratory photographs of obscure-looking phone-boxes from exotic locations around the globe. The idea of "jacking in" was like tapping into a virtual world but also like being a junky. "Jacking up" and "jacking in" contained the same meme of addictive fascination and danger, of accessing something forbidden and life-changing. We kept returning like addicts to the internet because each time we jacked in again, some new capability had appeared, some new digital territory had been colonised. We could operate a crane in a sandpit on the other side of the world. We could dress up avatars that would display on other people's computers. We could send messages on open chat channels. We could see web traffic coming from countries all over the world. Today, consumers have been led to expect to change and upgrade their connected devices every six months. In those early years, we got addicted to innovation, but it was anything but mainstream. At least part of our addiction was about differentiating ourselves. Our online habit was our particular rebellion. It was hard to see how it would transmute into mainstream consumerism.

Parallel universes - DVDs and the Internet

The internet would change the whole industry, but in its early years, commercial players in the entertainment industry did not see it generating revenue. They remained keen to pursue products on discs. For a music company like EMI, they were equipped to manufacture, distribute, and retail round bits of plastic in shiny boxes. The industry could retain control and achieve a more sophisticated product on disc than it could as yet online. While Philips' Digital Compact Cassette had failed, the Sony Mini Disc had been a success, it made clear commercial sense to pursue discs. DVDs came out in 1995 and could hold a whole movie. CD and DVD ROM discs were also the main driver of growth in computer games. Between 1993 and 1998,

34

the games industry was to become as large as the music industry with worldwide sales of video games growing from $19bn to $30bn. EMI had a significant interest in trying to license music into games and find new ways of raising revenues from this burgeoning sector.

In mid-1995, Spice Girls fever gripped the world and EMI CEO Ken Berry who had come from Virgin was celebrated as the cleverest man in the music industry. Under his direction, I was invited to move across from the alternative-minded Virgin labels to the rather more corporate EMI, home of altogether more conservative artists from a previous generation like the Beatles, Queen, Pink Floyd and a few newer acts like Blur and Radiohead. I reported to Shelagh Macleod who was also ex-Virgin and now ran Business Affairs worldwide for EMI. My role as Vice President New Media for EMI worldwide was completely new. Other major labels had someone in a role that included online and multimedia, but after some debate it was agreed that I should inhabit these parallel universes. Psychizophrenia was not the inevitable outcome, but it might have been.

The major German publishing house, Von Holtzbrink, had developed a Europe-wide reputation for CD ROM publishing. I flew frequently to Munich, to visit their interactive division, with whom EMI had a deal. We discussed the various ways we might produce titles together. Commercial obstacles abounded. We wanted to do a Guiness Book of Hit Singles on CD ROM, but the licensing was a nightmare. With Virgin Interactive Entertainment we tried to create games with bands like Blur and Radiohead. Either we could not get the music publishers to play ball and charge reasonable rates (they control rights to lyrics and compositions in a recording), or third parties with whom we were negotiating thought EMI was being too greedy in its royalty rate demands, which was undoubtedly the case. Record companies had a certain way of working and it generally involved trying to strike as aggressive and rapacious a commercial deal as possible. The more I looked at the CD ROM Multimedia projects I had inherited, some of which were games, some interactive books or reference works, the more convinced I was that they would never make the company any money and needed closing down. At that time, most of my projects involved spending absurdly large amounts of money on the wrong things and hardly anything at all on the right ones. But none of the Von Holtzbrink projects was as expensive as Queen the Eye.

The rock band Queen was all but defunct. The death of lead singer Freddy Mercury in 1991 had left the band looking around for new and inventive ways to make money out of a completed catalogue. EMI had made so much money out of Queen over the years that when their manager, the redoubtable Jim Beach, suggested to EMI CEO Rupert Perry that they were going to make a CD ROM game called The Eye, Perry had no option but to agree to bankroll the entire project. A year later, in 1995 when I inherited the project, the team had extended it to a 5 CD ROM set. Queen had created a development company with 50 developers and designers. Appropriately enough, the office was situated in the royal town of Windsor, nestling under the walls of Windsor castle, the Queen of England's weekend home. The game's storyline was simple. A future totalitarian regime had taken control of the world and banned all music from being played anywhere. The player's mission was to free the music and free the world. From a marketing point of view, this concept was nearly useless. None of the band members appeared in the game. While Queen's music would be used in the background and various characters from their song lyrics would come to life, the story was not related to Queen, the band at all. The project boasted good graphics and some rather creaky technology, which may have been innovative when the project started but was rapidly going out of date. The creative director had just left in a tantrum, the project was about 30% complete. The bill to EMI had reached £1 million. It took another nine months and some further £750,000 to wrestle the project to the ground. Eventually it came out and Electronic Arts sold about 12 copies. In order to save face, two years later, Toshiba EMI in Tokyo reluctantly squeezed out their Japanese language version too, but no one in Japan had anything to play it on. Copies of Queen, The Eye vanished without trace.

Back at Virgin Records, the company's summer '95, worldwide executive conference was held in the middle of the Arizona desert, at a resort called the Boulders, near Scottsdale. About a hundred Virgin executives arrived to celebrate their successes with global acts like the Rolling Stones (Voodoo Lounge Tour), Shaggy (Mr Boombastic), Neneh Cherry and Youssou N'dour (Seven Seconds). Once again, I presented the opportunities that the internet offered to music but no one knew what to do with that. That degree of change simply didn't fit the mindset. One evening, I wandered out into the desert with Ken Berry to discuss whatever this internet opportunity might look like. I was unprepared and he let me know that he simply couldn't find a fit for the internet into the business agenda he had to maintain. What I was talking about was too hypothetical, too remote from making money to be meaningful. He had to make decisions based on the next year or two at the most. He was interested to understand what the next decade might bring, but he wouldn't do anything to invest in it. There was no shareholder value to be had in this meddling with new technology. Silver might have been addicted to it, but nobody else needed to get too excited. We went horseback riding, hot air ballooning, we partied in the middle of the desert under the stars amid burning candles illuminating stacks of food, drink, chocolates and flowers. It seemed as if the music party would never end.

Fighting corporate culture was difficult, but the technology addiction was powerful. We persisted in our efforts at internet innovation. Having taken the first step connecting Virgin's offices to SuperJanet, the obvious next one was to connect up the rest of EMI. Part of my web fantasy was to webcast recording sessions from Abbey Road studios, live across the internet via the high speed, high quality UK backbone. More prosaically we thought of moving master recordings between A&R offices and the studios in split second time, enabling the whole of EMI's music catalogue to be flashed about West London at digital speeds inside our own high speed network - with complete security. With the help of our new friends at Videotron, we connected all four of the locations occupied by EMI at the time around London with a T1 fibre ring which as far as I know still exists. One side effect of this was that, driving to the office one morning, I found myself stuck in unusually bad traffic. As I crawled along Abbey Road and reached the studios, I saw the construction signs. "Videotron apologises for any inconvenience - cable laying underway". A year later, the studios were using the high bandwidth connection to relay high quality master recording files to EMI's European CD manufacturing plant in Hilversum, Holland. Thus saving the company courier costs and speeding up the album release cycle.

The massive gulf between technology and music represented a huge challenge to cross. Most of my addicted tampering with technology was seen as strategic at best and irrelevant to most people in the industry. Yet, the signs of efforts to align music and tech continued to grow. It was at this time, in 1996, that Steve Jobs famously returned to Apple Computer. He immediately set about repositioning the company as the most creative of any business in technology or consumer electronics. Under Jobs, the company created an Apple Masters programme, aligning themselves with leading creatives in the emerging fields of digital media, video games and CD ROM publishing. Peter Gabriel had already received critical acclaim for his Xplora and Eve projects. Both were art projects thinly disguised as games and Apple happily sponsored them. Apple understood that an art sensibility pointed the way ahead. Creative work created at the very edges of what is commercially viable would offer new thinking that the mainstream would never yield. Gabriel's Real World studio was busy spending Virgin Records' money alongside Apple's on making these beautifully conceived titles. They may have been non-commercial but Apple Computer was busily learning not just about working with artists but what innovation in music might mean. Apple decided to approach the music industry again and, in the context of the Beatles, this gave rise to certain issues. As early as 1991, Apple Computer and Apple Corps (the Beatles' production company) had been in court over the use of the brand name. Apple Corps insisted that Apple Computer could not enter the music business. The outcome of the lawsuit settled the demarcation boundaries between the two companies and the scope of the use of their respective trade marks. Apple Computer was not allowed to use the Apple brand in connection with music.

So when under Jobs' new direction, Apple approached EMI about establishing a DVD studio at its famous Abbey Road Studios, executives responded with some caution. Apple's interest vindicated those that believed in EMI's disc based business. Apple was strategically no further down the internet road than EMI. They read the market the same way and saw DVD production as a key part of the value chain. The only people who disagreed with the plan were the Beatles' production company, Apple Corps whose CEO at the time was the Beatles' old tour manager, Neil Aspinall. The Beatles had a strong association with Abbey Road, it was the name of the last album they ever recorded as a group. They were not going to allow this other Apple to set up an Apple Studio in Abbey Road that might for one minute look like it had any endorsement from their Apple Corps. If the Beatles' Apple Corp represented the highest standards of the music industry, McCartney, Harrison, Star and Yoko Ono representing the spirit of Lennon, embodied its most conservative values. Holding back against the advances of technology seemed to be the Beatles' consistent response to change.

Much negotiation ensued. Expensive dinners were hosted. Careful plans were hatched. The studio opened as the Abbey Road DVD Authoring Suite sponsored by Apple Computer. This sensitivity is even more ironic to recall, when one considers that within ten years, Apple was to become responsible for 85% of the global music industry's digital revenues through its iTunes stores, which opened in 2003.

The tables finally turned in 2006, when Apple Corp again tried to prevent Apple Computer's logo being used on the iTunes store and on iPods. On the 8th of May 2006, the BBC reported:

> The Beatles have lost their court challenge against Apple Computer over its iPod and iTunes download service. Sir Paul McCartney, Ringo Starr and the families of George Harrison and John Lennon control the Apple Corps label. They claimed the US firm broke a (1991) deal aimed at ensuring there would not be two Apples in the music industry. But Mr Justice Anthony Mann ruled that the computer company used the Apple logo in association with its store, not the music, and so was not in breach. The ruling means iPods and iTunes will still be able to carry the Apple name and logo.

The Beatles were one of the bands to hold out the longest against digital distribution, only allowing their music to be made available on iTunes in 2010. Throughout this entire period, of course, their music was readily available for digital download for free on unauthorised file-sharing services around the world.

Even once it became more acknowledged among label executives that the online world possessed great potential, opinion was still deeply divided. Some argued that the web worked best as a purely promotional channel, to be used for its marketing value only. Others saw that it offered entirely new ways of doing business. Publicists and promoters dished out tracks or pieces of music for web sites to give away for free while corporate lawyers worried about the precedents being set. In the past, giving music away had been a regular part of every music plugger's toolset, but doing it digitally was a whole different story. The lawyers hated it. They started to try to stop digital initiatives, more frequently and more desperately in order to preserve the status quo.

A major label has always wanted to control everything. That is the mindset. The label is in control. It makes stuff happen even when people don't know it. Record companies liked to be behind influential events and associated with the latest things. Whether they were linked to LiveAid, the World Cup or a general election, major label executives felt they were failing if they were not really close to the most fashionable aspect of anything in the national eye. As the internet grew in importance, the label stance shifted from instinctive denial to bargaining for dominance.

Domination is all about details and labels' lawyers love the minutiae. The internet provoked some of the most technically pedantic arguments around artists' domain names. Artists ended up with .com, co.uk, .net suffixed domains because one site was the band's, another was the label's and a third might be a fan site that got set up first. The URL that controls access to an artist's website would seem, on the face of it, to be a natural part of what an artist could expect to own as a core asset. But if the label paid for the site, its fancy tech bells and whistles, then the label argued, the url should belong to them. The labels couldn't decide if websites were like a promo video or more like tour support, but both were recoupable and the labels still wanted to own everything. There was discomfort at complicating factors such as that while a website was global only a few artists were signed globally, most had separate territorial deals. They gave little thought to artists' managers who might create direct revenue streams from selling tickets online or building their own fan online communities. Today, official social network pages and mobile apps have grown up alongside websites in the armoury of fan recruitment, but the battle continues between labels and artists as to who owns what aspect of their online presence.

The addictiveness of the internet drove innovators on in something like a race into a futuristic past. The science fiction writers like William Gibson, Bruce Sterling and Neal Stephenson fired imaginations with parallel worlds in which all of reality was reflected virtually but subtly changed. Much of the debate that would follow would be about whether to replicate on-line what exists in the real world or whether the web demanded an entirely new way of doing things. Our addiction grew as early adopters, we continuously explored the web's immense potential. The transition in strategic thinking that the labels and consumer electronics companies underwent was from thinking of the web as merely a new a distribution channel to thinking of it as an entirely new world. The truth in reality lies somewhere between the two. Stepping up to the debate about the web's strategic importance to businesses was not an even transition. It is still barely complete for music and for other creative sectors, the understanding has not even fully permeated. In 1993, books were in print, videos were on vhs and games were firmly on consoles. Two key technological innovations which happened to occur in that same year, would shift things on another gear.

2. Conspiring technologies

The mp3 audio compression standard (a global standard method for compressing audio digitally) and the MOSAIC web-browser were both launched in 1993. The coincidence of these two major developments in the same year was the key to massive change. The combination of these technologies enabled two important steps: the creation of a really small compressed music file that you could transmit quickly across low bandwidth modems and store in a solid state device, combined with an easily browsable website where you could offer files for download. In one year, two technologies coming from completely different contexts and developed with completely different motivations, laid the seeds for the substantial disruption of an entire industry. The advent of the mp3 and the web rendered digital music solid state, portable and instantly globally distributable. From that point on, websites grew like wildfire all over the internet and lots of them offered clips of music to download in mp3 format - legally or otherwise.

On a dingy, November afternoon in 1996, Larry Miller of AT&T Labs walked into my office in Gloucester Place with the first ever mp3 player to demonstrate. Held together with duct tape, it was a clunky-looking black box, built into an old Sony Walkman CD player. Most significantly it had no moving parts. Considering the importance of this breakthrough, the effect was surprisingly unsexy. Miller was on a mission to evangelise the player and the concept of the mp3 as a new standard. AT&T (along with the Fraunhoffer Institute in Germany and Thomson in France) were the original Mp3 patent owners. The player was a vital missing piece in the puzzle, the key to mobility. Everyone knows that the power of music is that it forms the soundtrack to our lives. Digital music had to break away from the tyranny of being tethered to the desktop. Miller's box was the forerunner of the iPod, but what it possessed in functionality, it lacked in style. Of course, this was simply a laboratory prototype, a proof of concept for the first time that music could be recorded onto a silicone chip and made mobile. Before Apple came to dominate the portable player market, plenty of other companies would explore the space, but like AT&T few of them considered the design or the form factor from the outset.

After Miller did his tour of the labels, it took another two years before the first commercially marketed mp3 player was produced by a company called Diamond Multimedia. The Diamond Rio was a small black box, the size of a dictaphone, weighing just a few ounces. It sat comfortably in the palm of the hand and it played mp3s. A cable connected the Rio to a desktop computer and some simple software allowed files to be transferred. A small monochrome LED screen on the device displayed the track information and a round pad supported the usual play, stop, forward and back transport controls. The Rio was simple and effective and instantly invoked the anger of the major labels. In 1998, their trade body, the Record Industry Association of America (RIAA), sued Diamond Multimedia, seeking to have the Rio banned. Their argument was that this Mp3 player was an incitement to infringe copyright. The case failed on a technicality of law, but the adventure around portable devices was just beginning.

Not long after that, Sony had two divisions, competing with each other, both producing digital music-players. Both worked with AACR2, a competing audio compress standard or CODEC to mp3 with slightly higher sound quality and both contained copy protection. Neither of these Sony players (one was called the Music Stick) would play Mp3 encoded tracks at all and they depended on encoding software on Sony laptops to transfer the music onto the portable player via a memory stick.

That set of design decisions, probably made under pressure from Sony Music, drove Sony Corporation from a position of market leadership with the Sony Walkman to market irrelevance with their new digital players.

In the event, the device that Miller showed me that day came to nothing. There was no way that AT&T Labs would productise it. Miller's prototype seemed too away far from their core business. Equally, the labels were simply not ready to acknowledge that a device like this could or should be licensed to deliver their music. Considering that AT&T in 2007, ended up negotiating with Apple to be the exclusive distributor at the launch of the revolutionary iPhone across the US, it is ironic that they didn't run with Miller's player. If they had paid closer attention to him, a few years earlier, it might have been ATT&T licensing the iPhone to Apple Computer not the other way around.

As soon as the the RIAA saw the Diamond Rio, they sued. They claimed that the Rio was an incitement to make copies and infringe the labels' copyrights. The RIAA had a problem though. Unlike games industry CD-ROMs which were securely linked to the games consoles and could not be easily ripped, Audio CDs did not have any copy protection on them. The "Redbook" Audio CD standard, created by Sony and Philips in the early 80s could have included some sort of copy protection, but for reasons still shrouded in history, the companies did not choose to adopt that option. The RIAA lost the case against the Rio. The problem of digital copying was of the music industry's own making. The Diamond Rio started something on the leading edge of technology that Apple would bring into the mainstream. It was not until early 2001, Apple added built-in CD writing drives to its desktop computers and adopted its famously provocative advertising campaign: Rip, Mix, Burn.

MP3.com

At this early stage in the development of the music industry's move online, mp3 was already the format of preference for most users of the new web, but it had not necessarily reach a point of market dominance. The Sony devices which used their own form of compression sounded better than mp3 and there were several other contenders to the crown; AAC and AACR2, OGG Vorbis, FLAC and of course Microsoft's Windows Media Audio (WMA). MP3 became the standard not because of its audio or even technical superiority. It became the standard because of its ease of use and because it was largely unencumbered by companies trying to layer copy protection methods on top of it. Californian entrepreneur Michael Robertson was one of the first to see the enormous potential of using Mp3s online. In late 1997, he launched mp3.com. It was a simple if idealisitic website which allowed any band, well known or unheard of, to post mp3s of their newly recorded tracks. Consumers could surf the site, browse the newest postings or most popular tracks, download and listen to them. The site levelled the playing field. On mp3.com, for the first time any recording artist could reach out directly to his or her audience and let them have the music. No third party distributor was required. Mp3.com looked superficially just like this new place to market your band but, a whole new kind of business emerged from it, an enabling platform that offered distribution easily and affordably when before it had been impossibly expensive and controlled by inaccessible multinational companies.

Robertson built a huge cult following, showing up at the numerous internet music conferences and laying into the luddite, fan-unfriendly music industry with a witty and campaigning spirit. His free market attitude, his customer focus and his persistent desire to disrupt the music industry kept him in pursuit of new features, new ways in which the combination of the web and mp3 could be more attractive to customers. He became the hero of the mp3 nation.

No wonder the major labels grew rapidly suspicious. The definition of a major label was that it ran its own manufacturing and controlled its own distribution and, by the way, they manufactured and distributed for the independent guys too - thus controlling 85% of the market. The conspiring technologies of mp3 and the web, embodied in the fledgling Mp3.com did away with both of those key components at a stroke. It took a stab at the heart of what defined them as majors.

As an advocate of change working within a label, I felt conflicted by these developments. On the one hand I had an obligation to my employer to support their approach. Increasingly however, I felt the excitement of the new. I sensed that the labels were losing an opportunity here, that the culture of change and forward-thinking innovation is the natural home of creative artists and therefore of those that publish them. Unbeknown to me, I would become personally involved in lawsuits against mp3.com and that personal sense of conflict would come even closer to the surface.

Project Madison

As the number of technology experiments increased around how to maximise the impact of the web and mp3, staff in the major labels began to realise that digital distribution was becoming a key battle ground. They were, however, loath to invest in new infrastructure let alone new technology that they were ill-equipped to understand. Shareholder profit and executive bonus remuneration operated to a much shorter time line than any of these new innovations. These were the priorities that dictated senior management thinking. Yet as time went by, digital distribution continued to become more central to the concerns of their teams and the lower down the pecking order, the younger the staff, the more insight was growing about the potential. Internal rivalry between IT directors, lawyers and heads of marketing and promotions grew. They turned into turf wars over who would take control of emerging internet strategy. This marked a critical period in the dawning recognition of the importance of the web to the business. So when, in 1997, IBM approached music industry heads in New York and offered to solve the internet problem for them, they jumped on it.

They called it the Madison project and its goal was simple and huge. Why it was called Madison I don't know, perhaps because it was driven by Sony Corporation whose headquarters are on Madison Avenue. The partners wanted to create the industry standard for the digital distribution of music over the internet. The anti-trust issues of even attempting a project like this were immense. The industry had to avoid any perception that it might be acting as a cartel. Yet to create a platform on this scale, they had to work together. The only legal solution was for IBM to run the whole thing, and for the labels to be individual and separate participants.

The IBM executives involved in Madison were in rock n roll heaven. This was the coolest IT project to end all cool IT projects. The record label executives were less certain. Project Madison was complex. Critically, as has been discovered by every consumer-facing music distribution service since, if you don't have all of the major catalogue in there, then you may as well not launch. Music fans don't care what label their favourite artists are on, they only care about their favourite artists.

Convoluted negotiations ensued between the five major, ego-driven record companies and IBM. Anti-trust paranoia and the belief that the existing model still had plenty of mileage left in it, made it hard to know what priority to give the project. Even being seen by music retailers like Tower Records or Best Buy to be thinking about this kind of development would create new friction with the retail community. No one imagined then that music retail might vanish altogether, let alone that the record companies might develop an industry-wide strategy which would result in its deliberate elimination. Each major area of policy was contentious. Digital Rights Management, transaction mechanisms, audio compression quality and choice, end playback systems, device control, CD-burning capabilities, the list went on. The big disruptive questions of internet commerce inevitably arose. Who should get paid if a piece of music belonged to a UK record label, but was sold from a French website, by a US Tourist using a Canadian credit card? Even as they worked on the parameters for this trial, the executives occasionally acknowledged that they were making industry policy on the fly while at other times the "test" nature of Madison served only to trivialise attitudes.

Sometimes Sony and Warner seemed to be in complete alignment about the way forward, working hard to bring the other three companies in line. At other times, the two lead majors seemed to be pulling in completely opposite directions. IBM executives spoke a completely different technical and business language from the music companies. They swore a lot less and made fewer jokes . But it didn't make for an easy conversation. Nobody exactly knew what was happening. The IBM guys paid for most of the development and the labels added cost as their requirements grew more complex. Despite intense efforts on all parts, towards the end of 1999, the Madison project eventually subsided under the weight of its own internal complexity.

*

In the autumn of 1998, the first dot-com bubble had almost reached the peak of its well- documented absurdity. At a party in Los Angeles' Pacific Palisades, all the guests were given rose-coloured paper "stock certificates" on arrival. We were told archly by the hostess that the IPO would be at midnight when everyone would be able to exercise their options. The whole of California was consumed by the bubble and by money raining down from investors. As one colleague put it: "all you had to do was shake the tree and money would fall out". People who had no business sense at all were suddenly talking about stock-options, warrants and equity as if everyone were a financial expert and always had been.

EMI transferred me to Los Angeles and we found a house in Studio City, twenty minutes commute from the Capitol tower. Our neighbour was Mike Post, the composer of theme tunes for Hill Street Blues and Law and Order (among many others). He was quiet, threw no wild parties and showed no interest in the internet either. Despite the rampant web euphoria, most of my new colleagues at Capitol Records weren't really any more into the internet than the guys in the UK - apart from the "web crew" who considered themselves to be way ahead of the curve. The office I was allocated was on the ninth floor of the Capitol Tower, the iconic stack-of-records building at the corner of Hollywood and Vine. The entrance hall was lined with signed, black and white photographs of Frank Sinatra, Dean Martin and the rest of the '50s brat-pack who had all recorded in the building's famous basement studio. During the period when EMI became the property of Citi Bank, the building was sold to the city of Los Angeles who leased it back to EMI. Subsequent to the sale of most of EMI to Universal, the lease has expired the building is being turned into luxury condominiums - a purpose to which the building is much better suited than offices. At that time, opposite the building, across Vine Street, was a parking lot of a large sound stage regularly used by MTV for auditions. Crowds of LA's aspiring talent would line up in the sun, around the block to try out for whatever particular show was being hired that day. I would watch them from my office, pondering how many of them would switch from buying CDs to digital downloads over the next few years.

The offices in the Capitol Tower were dominated by huge wooden desks that were bolted to the floor. They deigned to allow the staff to be seated at them. When the occasional earthquake lifted the whole building into the air and dropped it down again, it became apparent why it made sense to secure the desks in that way. My office had previously been occupied by the financial controller of Capitol Records. As the new media guy, there was a question mark over the legitimacy of my occupancy of this place. The human resources team had a hard time understanding that the internet warranted any importance in the hierarchy of a music company. The result of all this was that the layout of the office could not be changed in any way. Much the same could be said for the company's label structure and its approach to technology.

The Capitol building was dysfunctional and filled with a kind of craziness. Ken Berry, ex-head of Virgin, who had been promoted to head up EMI, the parent of Capitol had moved from London to take control of the US business directly, but the history of Capitol Records still dominated. The previous President had been Gary Gersh, his old office on the 13th or E Floor was kept permanently closed. Depending on which camp you were in, this was either because no one could possibly replace Gary and his passing was a tragedy from which Capitol Records would never recover. Or, for others this was more of a crime scene, permanently taped off by the authorities until the full scale of forensic evidence had been gathered and his guilt finally and scientifically proven. Gary Gersh represented that old pre-internet world and two camps at Capitol were either loyal to him or wanted him erased from history. The pressure that the internet was putting on the industry could be felt palpably within the companies themselves. There were tensions between those who were in complete denial about the significance of online music and those that were keen to dominate it utterly. There were tensions between those who wanted to go with the openness and the flow of sharing online and those that wanted to impose copy protection in as powerful and systematic way as possible.

SDMI

As industry torch-bearer or lead rottweiler (depending on your perspective), the Recording Industry Association of America (RIAA) was unremitting in its search for visible, robust solutions to the growing woes of its members. Out of the ashes of Project Madison came something even more ambitious, the Secure Digital Music Initiative (SDMI). It became clear that the labels couldn't control the world by building a platform with IBM. The problem required a larger solution, not so much a platform, more an entire architecture. A framework was needed that would allow music to be distributed securely across the internet and connect directly into playback devices without being stolen. The mp3 horse may have bolted, but that wouldn't stop the RIAA seeking to build a whole new stable.

Cary Sherman is a dapper, charming man and chief lawyer to the RIAA, based like all lobbyists in Washington DC. In late 1998, he convened a meeting of something called the SDMI Foundation. The founder directors represented each of the major labels. I was there for EMI. SDMI was an audacious project. Under its banner the music industry summonsed a meeting of all of the world's leading IT, audio and consumer electronics companies to join in trying to create a digital final solution on an unprecedented global scale. Leonardo Chiariglioni, a loquacious, somewhat patrician Tuscan was drafted in to oversee proceedings. He had built his career at Telecom Italia, spoke seven languages including Japanese and had been part of the Motion Pictures Expert Group who had developed the Mp3 standard in the first place. He seemed like the perfect figure to broker a new world order for music.

Chiariglioni presided over the SDMI proceedings like a papal emissary. He sat centre stage, while some of the world's leading digital experts made earnest submissions, imploring proposals for solutions, impassioned yet tedious explications of complex technological designs. Several hundred delegates attended the meetings, massed ranks of corporate representatives. Sony, Philips, IBM, CISCO, Intel, Microsoft, Oracle, Panasonic, Toshiba, Dolby and more, sent delegates along with the five music majors, the occasional indie and a scattering of start-up hopefuls. The label guys swaggered in wearing jeans and t-shirts under sports jackets, a few men still had ponytails. The tech guys were in suits or blue shirts and beige chinos with highly polished black shoes. The technology companies were huge, far more diversified than any of the music companies. The labels were pygmies amongst giants. To say that there was a culture clash between these guys didn't even begin to describe it. Apple Computer who might have bridged the gap was notably absent from the proceedings and Michael Robertson who despite his great insights into the problem was persona non grata. He organised a way cooler Mp3 Summit to rival SDMI in his native San Diego, which no one from a major label could have even attended without risking their job.

Were the technologies conspiring? It certainly seemed that the technologists might be. In the buzzy corridors around the SDMI negotiating chamber, a nervous paranoia ruled. Small groups of executives from different companies clustered together and others observed, drawing all kinds of conspiracy theory conclusions from seeing who was talking to whom. Masters of the web and the mp3 were well represented, but the thought leaders in SDMI were Philips Labs and Universal Music. Newcomers with smart ideas about copy protection were there too, in particular a company called Intertrust led by the technology evangelist Talal Shamoon. The Intertrust folk invested heavily in the process, trying to create a realistic framework, that was viable and implementable. As a representative of a start up technology business that wanted to play nice, Shamoon was the bright young thing who half - realised that he was uniquely positioned to gather consensus across all these rivalrous companies. Intertrust also saw in SDMI the opportunity to embed their super-distribution technology in the very heart of this new secure, global standard. They recognised the innate fluidity of content on the web and wanted to go with the flow. Intertrust's notion that each consumer could also be a retailer was radical and ambitious. They wanted to design SDMI's architecture to enable that new model. As well as simply securing the content, they wanted to make it go viral too.

Except perhaps in the so-called free "sharing economy", we have yet to see that ambition realised.

The largest of all the majors by 1999, was the Polygram group of labels, its ownership was complex and troubled. Majority owner, Philips of Eindhoven, had floated a small percentage of the company on the US stock market and also accepted an investment from MCA Matsushita (aka Panasonic). Philips had a strong commercial incentive to sell music content because selling content helped to sell more record players and CD players. If you were selling a music player, it would be good to have some music to sell with it. Once digital music went online, their traditional business logic was disrupted. The mp3 and the web made music something that could be played on a computer and on the new portable devices.

As the business strategists at Philips looked at the future, they would have been justified in thinking that they might have achieved as much as they could and that now was a good moment to exit. The cooperation of Sony and Philips over the standard for CDs in the early 1980s had created the massive CD market, but this was not to be repeated in the face of Mp3 which was becoming increasingly associated with free music. In 1999, Philips sold their entire recorded music group to Seagram (Canada's largest drinks company). The effect was a critical disconnection of hardware from software. Once Philips no longer retained any commercial incentive to protect music content, only Sony remained as a vertically integrated business with the capability of creating a perfect market by controlling the way consumers accessed the music produced by their record company on the devices manufactured by their consumer electronics division. It would not be until November 2001 that the relationship between hardware and music would be radically reorganised via the internet in a way which shifted the power away from recorded music companies and firmly into the hands of one technology company, Apple Computer. The seamless easy-to-use model connecting the iPod and iTunes created a new market for music and set the model for app stores and the sale of other digital media ever since. Before all of that could come about though and while SDMI continued its global meetings in airport hotels around the world, the music industry was about to face the biggest challenge of free that it had ever met.

Napster

In June 1999, Sean Parker and Sean Fanning launched Napster, a file sharing website that changed the world. The free peer-to-peer service offered the entire world's music collection for free. It liberated tracks from albums and allowed bootleg recordings to sit alongside commercial releases. It was more comprehensive than any record store could ever be. Napster unleashed music from corporate control and spawned a whole new generation of ideas about how to access music. It gained instant notoriety and heightened the RIAA's demonisation of mp3. I found Napster incredibly exciting. Although its interface only offered basic functionality, Napster was the best music product the world had yet seen because of the simple, instant availability of any piece of music you could name. It removed any friction of transaction because in its case there was none, but it set the precdent for one-click purchasing that would be replicated on all the commercial services that followed. Napster didn't try to impose anything, it just offered the music - all of it - no complications. Its launch issued the single greatest challenge ever to the viability of the music industry.

Napster put the major labels on the ropes. It had the potential to create immense new audiences and new revenues, just as CDs were starting to fade from their sales peak. Paid for access to the Napster platform could have easily been created. A subscription fee could have been charged of users to make all the music available and since the peer-to-peer technology cleverly used the computing power of consumers' own machines, running costs were lower than those of centralised download services. In many respects, the secret of Spotify's success today is modelled on the original Napster platform. Peer to peer (P2P) technology is at the heart of Spotify's lower cost streaming engine. If the music industry had chosen to embrace the change that Napster signalled then, it might have leapt forward rapidly and lucratively. Instead the world had to wait for another nine years before Spotify eventually launched in 2008.

The industry response to Napster was the inevitable litigious attack - this time with clear justification. This was blatant copyright infringement on an unprecedented scale. The pressure grew on the digital strategists in the boardroom of every major label to come up with a realistic industry alternative and fast. The music companies still believed that they could stay in control of this market. They just needed the right tools, the right agreements, and maybe some new legislation. In the minds of the consumer electronics's business developers, the trickle of mp3 content to play on their new digital audio players had just become a flood. The single mp3 horses that had bolted the stable, just became a wild herd galloping over the hill.

At SDMI, the appearance of Napster created a kind of desperation. On the one hand the labels' need for a positive outcome had been significantly intensified. On the other, the consumer electronics and information technology companies understood that Napster and its undoubted successors would provide them with a significant new stream of content without the need for any deal with the music companies. The commercial incentive to tie music sales to device sales had been severely undermined. Now the music companies had to compete with free.

A critical meeting was scheduled for September 1999, at the art deco, Park Lane Hotel in London. One final proposal would be placed on the table. The UK was experiencing one of its glorious Indian summers. The meeting room was small and poorly ventilated, the walls covered in bevelled mirrors reflecting multiple views of troubled music executives' faces. The labels argued aggressively that Napster would be put down by litigation and that such services would never be allowed to blight the market. In response, the device manufacturers offered a deal. They would cooperate with the music companies and create a secure channel. It would only allow the music to pass from a computer to the device if payment had been made. In exchange, the music companies had to agree to give up any claims against private copying. Consumers would be allowed to make as many private copies of a track as they wished, so long as they purchased it through the secure SDMI channel first. One more thing though, all the music that was ripped from CDs would also have to be playable and the SDMI channel would not be able to prevent its circulation around the internet. Internet service providers and network operators were not present at SDMI. That was a whole separate problem to consider.

In the negotiating room, the atmosphere was intense. What had begun as a congenial assemblage of bright techies with innovative ideas, had become a sharply pointed commercial debate. Sony might have achieved a better deal, but they had little strength or coherence. The Sony consumer electronics divisions in Tokyo competing with each other and neither of them speaking with the recorded music company in New York. The RIAA's chief dealmaker, Sherman tried to guide and advise the labels. Taking his lead was much easier than trusting one another even then, but none had the stomach for this deal. It flew in the face of basic music industry policy principles. They simply could not accept the precedent that would be set by accepting a loss of control over private copying. There were too many lawyers in the room. The labels rejected the proposal. SDMI was finished. In the face of the commercial might of the world's computer and consumer electronics manufacturers on the one hand and the radical opportunism of Napster on the other, the labels had tied themselves to the sinking ship of their old business model. They would see its value diminish year on year by over 50% during the next ten years as CD sales fell off a cliff and digital music sales only gradually began to fill the void.

SDMI's failure was part of a subtle shift in global approaches to commercial technology development, driven at least in part by burgeoning dotcom entrepreneurialism. The development of the Redbook Audio CD standard by Sony and Philips, the mp3 compression standard developed by AT&T, Thomson and the Frauhofer Institutes of Germany, and the DVD standard from Warner and Toshiba, were products of a collaborative approach to R&D. This era of multinational corporate collaboration lasted from the early 80s to the mid-90s. SDMI may have been rightly criticised for being an arrogant attempt on the part of the music industry to try to regain global control of its market. Yet SDMI also had a kind of old-fashioned academicism. Senior technical folk did genuinely trade in ideas with one another and were committed, openly and collaboratively to trying to arrive at a solution to securing media for commerce on the internet. A curious combination of academic indulgence and music industry luxury showed up in the romantic locations of the meetings: Kyoto, Hawaii, Florence, London. While the hubris of the music industry was largely to blame for the practical failure of SDMI, it was also a victim of a broader shift in values. The dot-com era saw companies breaking away from that kind of collective standard setting and market creation.

Despite the continued efforts of national governments and the European Union to encourage collaborative R&D and knowledge transfer from universities, dot com entrepreneurialism drives a fundamentally individualistic approach. Academic research had led to the development of Mosaic, a stumbling prototypical web browser and this in turn led to the commercial development of Netscape. Yet, during the late 1990s, as the dot-com bubble grew, so-called "browser wars" broke out between Netscape and Microsoft's Internet Explorer, the major corporate battled the internet start-up for market dominance. In 1998, Netscape was acquired by America Online for $4.2bn and the United States Department of Justice prosecuted Microsoft for monopolistic practices in a court case that would roll on for the next eight years. These were early indicators of a shift to an era of more atavistic entrepreneurialism and aggressive corporatism. When Philips sold off its software interests to concentrate on hardware, it may have had an insight into the unsustainability of the old music industry model, but perhaps it was also shifting to a more aggressive, less collegiate corporate strategy. More recently in 2012, global patent wars of litigation have broken out between Apple and Samsung, while Google aggressively entered the mobile land-grab by acquiring Motorola Mobility for $12.5bn, largely for its wealth of mobile-related patents. Collaborative R&D, in the late 1980s and early 1990s, brought companies together in consortia of shared commercial interest. That was the era of big corporate research labs, but the internet became the lab. Internet entrepreneurs became the researchers. The role of the corporations was to spot the promising company and acquire it whatever the price. The dot-com era pitted giant corporations against one another in winner-takes-all type gladiatorial contests that have become today's prevailing ethos, spurred on by the increasingly aggressive and short-termist demands of the capital markets.

Individualistic entrepreneurs were the ones that built the really disruptive models.

3. SORCERER'S APPRENTICES

Entrepreneurs were the sorcerers' apprentices of the dot-com bubble. As the RIAA pursued the industry-wide strategic effort of SDMI, more near-term deal opportunities presented themselves to the labels on a daily basis in the City of Angels. A seemingly endless succession of venture-capital-backed entrepreneurs came down from Silicon Valley in Northern California to approached the labels in LA. EMI engaged eagerly with them all to pick their brains and learn about what novel directions the technologists were inventing. The technology companies were looking for licenses to use the labels' music in their new web-based services. The industry term for them was "supplicant" companies as a reflection of the old-world power imbalance between them and the labels. A friendly welcome was generally precursor to the savage stitch up of the deal terms. This kind of licensing became a regular and significant revenue stream for the major labels. The senior vice presidents of new media were targeted with quarterly multi-million dollar quotas to gather in through licensing, regardless of or sometimes because of the questionable sustainability of the businesses paying out.

They came from all over the US. They would walk in with their beige mid-West Chinos, neat white shirts, polished shoes and side partings, or shiny Chicago suits with pointy-toed shoes or from Texas with slightly sharper jackets and of course the cowboy boots and, if they came from San Francisco, they were their own walking cliches in sneakers, jeans and t-shirts. They were cash heavy with fresh funding from venture capitalist investment. So EMI's attitude was to soak them for as much cash as possible. Like many corporate entrepreneurs, I tried to manage the tricky balance of pursuing genuine personal interest and advancing corporate avarice.

Entrepreneurs' inventiveness was in full bloom. Every conceivable business plan for music came across my desk during those months. Streaming subscription services, a-la-carte download, rent to buy, kiosks for in-store CD-burning, kiosks for filling your mp3 player, disposable thumb drives the size of a matchbox preloaded with a single album, hard drives containing all the music in the world in a single box. The range of ideas and the craziness of some of what we saw was unprecedented. Interestingly, a lot of the ideas collectively brainstormed in that early flowering were barely feasible then, but subsequent technology advances (like wifi, bluetooth, always on broadband, etc), today they are possible and the business models are in the process of being worked on. In that first phase though, the game was about which entrepreneur could come up with the most disruptive technology and which label could come up with the most outrageous deal. Exploit or be exploited - the power tussle went back and forth.

Hollywood loves to negotiate through agents and lawyers and they have developed a common language. When they offer a deal, look carefully because it's all about some of the most disingenuous body language to be found in the commercial world. First, lean forward, shoulders hunched, head slightly to one side, as if resigned to an inevitability. Next, ensure your hands are out-spread, palms up to imply honesty. Lips must be pouting to suggest genuine thoughtfulness and a weighing of the pro's and con's. Then when the deal is laid out on the table, offer a simple shrug and say: "What's not to like"? The actual deal terms were invented on the spot every time, but there were always the same two or three key components. The first component was a cash advance - three quarters of a million dollars or so as a "catalogue access fee". One of the benefits of this for the labels was that this money would not be shared with their artists because it would not be attributable to any actual transactions. The second component would be a significant share of the revenue, a disproportionately unfavourable 80-20 split favour would be the usual opening offer. Woe betide any tech company that suggested that they might take a share of a label's revenues. It would be a long time before that would be allowed and even when it happened, it was in the guise of a retail split going to Apple for sales in the iTunes store - not for the technology! God forbid! The third element was a requirement to own a piece of the supplicant company. Again an opening demand would be very high, say 20% or 25% of the equity in the business. Any suggestion that the ownership might come in the form of something that needed to be earned out or set against actual performance in delivering music to the company, like an option would be summarily dismissed.

The label would also try to minimise the extent to which the artists themselves might benefit from this kind of deal. The intriguing idea that the data generated by new services might inform the label about what had been played by whom, was summarily rejected despite its obvious marketing value. This was another example of how the prospect of long term strategic benefit was sacrificed to financial short term gain. It might be useful to understand what consumers listening patterns or video viewing patterns might look like, but if the label didn't know what music had been played where, then it couldn't report that back to the artists or and it would not be in a position to share any of the associated revenue with the artists. Financial gain for the label at the expense of the artist seemed like a canny tactic at the time.

While there was not much competition between the label and the artists because the artists were always the last to get paid, there was not much competition between the labels either. The law in the US and the UK has always been very strict about anti-trust, ensuring that large multi-nationals should not act in concert and remain at all times competitive with one another. Journalists had long suspected that the major record companies formed a cartel controlling entry to the market, exploiting artists and dictating terms to retailers. Lawyers at the major labels were always scrupulous in maintaining their companies' record in such matters. They were also very clever at finding the ways to avoid anti-trust provisions.

The other key element in all of these new EMI deal terms was the inclusion of a "Most Favoured Nations" (MFN) clause. This clause said that no matter what deal terms were set out in this agreement, if the company made a better deal with another label then EMI would be entitled to know about it and benefit from it too. The majors could not act in concert and demand the same terms as a competitor, but if all the majors included a most favoured nations clause, then it guaranteed that the technology company partner would be forced to give them all the same terms without their ever asking. (In Europe, this practice has recently been banned by the EU as part of its negotiations with Vivendi/Universal over the 2012 acquisition of EMI).

Although for the most part the labels dictated terms to their artists, there were a cadre of superstar act whose success allowed them to turn the tables. The biggest names in music were attractive enough and rich enough to hire good lawyers that they wanted to control their digital rights along with other key deal terms. So finally, having set all those other comprehensively exploitative criteria for the right to license the vast majority of the music catalogue, in one final, insouciant, shrug of the shoulders, the label would casually drop into the conversation the fact that, of course, the major names such as the Beatles or the Stones, Queen or Janet Jackson would all be the subject of separate, individual negotiations. The chances were, that those artists were just not going to leave the building - unless it was for a lot more money again.

One of the earliest deals to be done in that era was for video streaming and it was with the company who produced Launch magazine. Launch had been a CD ROM publication and morphed smoothly into a seminal music website. It also spawned an interactive radio site called Launchcast, which allowed the first interactive music stations to be create amidst much controversy about how much interactivity would be permissible. Launch was run by Dave Goldberg who had previously been at Capitol Records. Hugely likeable, Goldberg was a past master at negotiating Hollywood-style. He'd been at it since birth. EMI eventually struck a deal with Goldberg for one of the first ever video streaming licenses, but not without the characteristic degree of shoulder hunching, pouting, screaming and finger pointing. His company was purchased by Yahoo! in 2001 for US$12 million. LAUNCH.com was later integrated into Yahoo! Music. Launchcast continued an uneasy and litigious relationship with the labels for another six or seven years as the majors continued to argue against the degree to which the music could be available entirely on-demand. David Goldberg eventually left Yahoo to become the CEO of SurveyMonkey. He is married to Sheryl Sandberg COO of Facebook.

Despite the delightful nature of the terms, many deals were done. The tech companies were eating out of the corporate hands; for the labels is was like taking candy from children. No wonder that the animosity between North and Southern California would only increase over the years. There were a lot of VCs who had feathered the bonuses of music industry executives in that period. The progress of the web is littered with multi-million dollar failed investments in music start-ups. As the dotcom bubble increased in pace throughout 1999, the labels' revenues continued to climb higher than they'd ever been.

Another group of sorcerers apprentices who were making money out of the web were commercial conference organisers. A wide variety of events took place in capital cities across North America and Europe. Executives from major labels and entrepreneurs from start ups, talked confidently about the massive disruptive effects of the new technology. We honed our discourse. We refined our futurist prophetic phrases. We laid out strategies and discussed paradigm shifts. With charm, and smoke and mirrors, music industry new media executives portrayed the major labels as approachable and innovative, while entrepreneurs provoked and mocked the lumbering slowness of the dinosaur companies. These events were spectator sports. There was genuine debate and real disagreement - emotions would often run high. In the years that followed, as it became more imperative on entrepreneurs to buddy up to executives who might turn out not simply to be licensors but also customers, the discussions have become more polite. The business has grown up, the debate is less adolescent, it may be a bit sterile now too.

Of course these events have always been for networking and moving deals forward as much as for corporate tub-thumping. At one such conference, held at the charmless Omni Hotel in downtown LA, I stumbled across entrepreneur, Raju Puthukarai. He was a former president of the Bertelsmann group's Music Club - a discount mail order business that schlocked out distressed inventory close enough to its currency period to make it attractive to consumers without upsetting the old retail trade too much. All the majors had this kind of extremely profitable music club offering. They regularly advertised 3 CDs for the price of 1 in the backs of the Sunday supplements. Puthukarai was working the conference floor, handing out the red herring (public offering prospectus) for his company Musicmaker.com. Its NASDAQ IPO was scheduled for the following week. Musicmaker had a very simple business model. They allowed consumers to go to their website, browse their listings of songs, choose their favourite thirteen tracks, which they would then burn to a CD and mail to your home.

There had been the beginnings of a deal between EMI and Musicmaker back in London, negotiated two years previously by then EMI COO, Roger Faxon. But nothing had come of it. Now Puthukarai was preparing to take the company public on the back of the dotcom boom. Back at the Capitol Tower, my newly installed boss Jay Samit picked up the information with alacrity. Samit relished the entrepreneurial opportunity that the bubble afforded. EMI persuaded Musicmaker to pull their IPO on the basis that EMI would invest in their company and make them much more valuable. The label then proceeded to pull off one of the most excessive music deals in the history of the first dotcom bubble.

The deal was very simple. EMI would license to Musicmaker all of EMI's catalogue (subject to 'artists consent') in exchange for 50% of the company's equity. By any normal standard the deal terms made little sense. Everyone understands that running any kind of consumer facing music service, requires all the music, not just one label's offering however good the catalogue might be. If EMI took 50% stock ownership, there simply wouldn't be enough of the company left to license catalogue from any of the other labels. Furthermore the deal took no account of the publishing agreements that MusicMaker would have to strike to complete the permissions necessary to use the content. Savvy entrepreneur though he was, Puthukarai may not have even realised that publishing was missing and Bob Bernardi, the CEO certainly didn't seem to care. Their model was still the old school music club which had always functioned out of the back door of a label. To these two old-timers, this seemed no different from many of their other label deals except that here was the frothiest IPO market anyone could remember in which uninformed consumers were day-trading on internet stocks like they were in Vegas.

Six months later, The London Times reported that the IPO raised over $400m. EMI cashed out a large piece of its "investment" on the day of the launch and after tax netted some $80m profit on the deal without having provided a single digital track to Musicmaker.com. Samit became EMI's dotcom hero and went on to mastermind a number of other similarly rapacious deals. All this, despite the fact, that there were only primitive means inside EMI to deliver digital tracks to MusicMaker. Part of the lobby on the 9th floor started to fill up with crates of CDs from the more compliant labels which were to be shipped to Musicmaker's offices. Not only was EMI making all the money, but under the terms of the deal Musicmaker agreed that they would digitise the label's entire catalogue and return a digital file of every track for EMI to use in whatever service it wanted - even in ones that would ultimately compete with Musicmaker. EMI at that time did not, however, have any centralised digital asset store in which to store such a set of tracks let alone redistribute them.

Not surprisingly perhaps, within two years of its IPO, the company went bust amid accusations of individual fortunes being made in sweetheart, "friends and family" stock trading deals. Musicmaker and its directors were the subject of a number of class action suits on the part of lawyers representing day-trading consumers. They claimed to have been misled by the company on its ability to deliver its service. In particular, there was a serious question over the likelihood of any of the most sought-after EMI content ever being useable. In a document dated September 20th 2001, the first of the class actions demanded a trial by jury. No such trial ever took place.

Musicmaker and the executives behind it were not typical. They were more music industry than technology focussed. They were more knowing. Many of the technology entrepreneurs were remarkably ignorant of the complexity of the rights issues in music. They mostly held simplistic views of what music and internet technology could do together. While their naivety was sometimes met with derision by label executives, the one thing that they could all see for certain was that once the mp3 genie was out of the bottle, there was no putting it back. The combination of the appetite of the NASDAQ market and the easy accessibility of the web itself encouraged wild-west entrepreneurship. It lowered barriers to entry and for many bright young technologists, the vision the internet offered was rich in opportunity which could be delivered through almost overnight transformation. The first dot-com bubble spawned many of the ideas that it has subsequently taken another twenty years to work into reality. In the story of the sorcerer's apprentice, the magic that the young wizard conjures up rapidly goes out of control. At the end of the tale, the old sorcerer returns and restores order in a normative move designed to put centuries of readers' minds at rest. Youthful enthusiasm so the folk tale goes, will always need tempering and managing by the experience of years. On the internet, the old sorcerer still seems very unlikely to return.

The first entrepreneurial challenge to the domination of record companies in the UK, came even before the bubble had inflated. In 1995, an energetic, anarchic entrepreneur called Ricky Adar created a company named Cerberus. It was in the business of creating the first properly configured, ready-to-roll-out digital distribution service for music. Inevitably, at first it did not boast much music. None of the labels would even consider the concept of licensing Adar's service. He had digitized some music, created the system to allow its distribution across the web and was demonstrating it to anyone who cared to look. If he had managed to deploy it, he would have scared the living daylights out of the majors. Adar scored a double page spread in the Sunday Times announcing his plans to transform the way that music was distributed globally. It was an impressive splash, but in a pattern that was to become very familiar, the major labels simply refused to pay Cerberus any attention. They were in complete denial. As far as they were concerned, this was not a conversation they need even contemplate.

Adar's entrepreneurial spirit remained undeterred. Like many others, he turned to the concept of in-store CD burning. In the entire five-year period of the first Internet bubble, more versions of this proposition were proposed to major labels than any other. The concept of retail music on-demand had the strategic attraction that it took an interesting incremental step toward virtual retail without fundamentally altering the record companies' core business model. Faced with the non-cooperation of the major music owners, Adar pivoted his business and did a deal with the Levi's store on Regents Street in London's premiere shopping district the West End, to offer custom CD burning exclusively for Levi's customers. It made Levis look leading edge (they were offering custom jean-cutting at the time too). A few independent labels licensed their music, after all it would still end up on disc, but the service never found a real consumer market. The evolution of digital distribution to record stores was simply too expensive and too late. Record stores would become almost extinct before digital distribution and in-store burning could come to the rescue. Mp3 file sharing and downloading would overtake the need for music on CDs at all.

The internet clearly changed the way executives felt about business in a very direct and emotional fashion. Experienced folk started to jump ship in the mid-nineties and leave the safety of the corporate world to enter the entrepreneurial life of the start-up company. New companies with exotic new internet names mushroomed. Yet, despite the allure of crazy IPOs and exits, leaving the comfort and security of the corporate world for a start-up was still seen as a brave step. Employees in the music industry enjoyed an ambience of affluence, high salaries, cushy benefits and lots of perks to the job. Of course there were those who were pushed out, but among the people starting to look more closely at online opportunities, the defectors started to grow in number. In the US particularly, the ready availability of investment finance, was the pull - venture capital got more and more keen. Defectors were regarded by ex-colleagues with a mixture of admiration and disdain. Admiration - because any comfortable corporate executive assures himself or herself that they possess a degree of security, which may be more illusory than real, but which certainly, has a contractual robustness that ensures a good safety-net. Despite the growing tide of venture funding in that period, it was still a brave step to leave the corporate mothership. Those who remained on the inside expressed disdain because the more the defections grew, the more start-ups challenged the norm. The tribe of technologists was increasingly challenging the tribe of music industry executives and the battle lines were beginning to be drawn up.

In mid-1996, somewhere on the Swiss border an affable Frenchman called Francois Xavier Nuttall (FX for short) was working with some forward-thinking cable guys. Nuttall had developed his own notion that music excited consumers more than anything else online and that digital distribution of music over a cable network would be a good new way for the new cable-delivered internet service to acquire customers. FX had developed a proprietary music player which could act as a front end for the service. Where did the music reside? How was it accessed? How was it to be discovered? He had none of these answers but a trial would help us find out. He convinced the French cable company to supply the player to all its customers for the opening screens of their internet service.

Nuttall wanted EMI to license him lots of music to populate the trial. We thought this seemed like an interesting model and agreed to explore it. At the same FX, wanted to lure me into joining with him in his new company. He needed someone who understood the labels and who could deliver music and artists. I was intrigued. No one had offered me a job in a start-up with equity before. Equity and what it meant was still a somewhat obscure financial services world term. Nonetheless, I began to feel the pull of the entrepreneurial opportunity. There was a freedom to innovate and a chance to make a real difference. Those were the things that were attractive about it - equity, even then, seemed a little illusory.

74

Unfortunately, Nuttall jumped the gun and got over excited about his prospects. Maybe he thought he could bounce EMI into licensing the project or maybe he was just naive. Before discussions had reached anything like a term sheet, Nuttall was talking rather breathlessly to the Financial Times. The story that EMI was about to partner with a French cable company appeared on the front page.

Senior management of EMI were not amused. Sir Colin Southgate, the company Chairman was on the war path. I was summonsed to be told: "We're not about to license our music to anyone, least of all a bunch of French cable operators. That is not the business we are in. We will never be in the business of making our music digital and degrading its value dramatically, as long as we are continuing to sell CDs. Are you completely out of your mind?"

The tirade of denial was intense. Whether this was positioning or genuine was hard to tell. Southgate had run a technology company before he ran EMI. He certainly had more than an inkling of where this was going and may privately have conceded that the company needed to embrace technology. Ideally, however, speculative research is not carried out on the front pages of international newspapers. The deal was not to be done and no EMI executive jumped ship to join that enterprise on that occasion. Nuttall was not repentant. He continued to work in the music industry with his start-up company which continued to develop the music player.

As the dotcom bubble reached its peak and when every self-respecting musician wanted to be associated with some new web project, FX got Phil Collins to write him an endorsement.

Today, still known as FX, Nuttall is one of the world's leading experts on music industry meta-data systems. He recently left a role as a senior adviser to CISAC (Conference International des Societees des Auteurs et Composeurs - the world organisation for collective rights management organisations) - to join the start-up of all start-up's, Google, whose relationship to music and the entertainment industry continues to be challenging and innovation-led - a sorcerer's apprentice to the old wizard.

The US dot-com hero of music in this heady era, was Michael Robertson. MP3.com was more than a business it was a project to disrupt the music industry repeatedly, terminally. Robertson's strategy was far more calculating and well conceived than Shawn Fanning's. Despite Napster's high profile and public heresy, Robertson was actually more inventive, more commercially and politically savvy. Robertson continued to innovate around what the technology, the web and the mp3 could do together. He did so in ways which continually provoked the RIAA and enticed consumers to expect more of music online. At its peak, mp3.com delivered in excess of 4 million mp3 audio files per day to over 800,000 unique users. The site achieved a customer base of 25 million registered users. Robertson would take mp3.com to the public markets with an IPO, in July 1999 and raise over $370 million. At the time, this was the single most profitable technology IPO ever. Alanis Morissette was an early investor in the site after it sponsored one of her tours. She owned nearly 400,000 shares in the company and her profit from the venture topped $3.4 million dollars at her exit.

So while he was excited by what mp3.com could mean for independent artists, he also wanted to add more services for more users. In 2000 he launched a new service called MyMp3.com which was designed to allow music consumers to stream the contents of CDs they had already purchased to desktops wherever they happened to be. Today, Apple's iTune's Match offers this service, but MyMp3.com looked to the majors like a clear test of how much disruption they would tolerate. They did what they knew best. They sued to close the site down and succeeded on a technicality.

Uplister Inc - a case study in entrepreneurship

By late 1999, my own discomfort at working in a label had grown pretty unbearable. The rumour mill around a possible EMI/Warner merger grew in seriousness and the lack of investment continued in the deals EMI was making with technology companies. California was awash with technology opportunities on offer on all sides and EMI showed no commitment. The job offers started to come in, both from other labels and from entrepreneurs.

An interesting new business was being set up by Universal and Bertelsmann Music Group, called PressPlay. It was one of two industry-owned attempts to set up its own online presence (the other was called MusicNet). An impressive CEO, Andy Nibley, had been hired from Reuters to run the company and it would be based in New York city. He flew me back east to meet him and colleagues. They had interesting plans. They were recruiting good people, but joint corporate ownership would hamper their operations, prevent them from responding effectively to competition. Nibley offered me a position and we enthusiastically discussed how it might all work. At the same time, I was talking to a Silicon Valley start-up who had much more radical ideas.

Most of the job offers from technology companies, were not worth taking. The degree of ignorance and naivety about the music industry was not surprising. But one team of engineers from San Francisco did appeal, precisely because they were so classically geeky and had little understanding of the music industry. The team was led by Toni Schneider a Swiss-German who had emigrated to San Francisco years earlier and Mike Taylor who hails from Columbus, Ohio. They had great technology company pedigrees and business development brains.

Both had worked together at a chip design company previously. They had pitched me with a concept a few months earlier, but their first idea sucked. Then they came back with a new concept, which was really exciting. They had intelligence and persistence. These guys would be good to work with. They placed a positive value on me too and were prepared to raise a round of financing in order to offer me a contract and sponsor my visa application. The VC, Andy Rappaport from August Capital, flew down from Sand Hill Road for us to meet. I had to weigh up the PressPlay offer from Nibley with its chance to work in New York or the offer from Schneider and Taylor to move to San Francisco. I decided to leave EMI and join the Bay Area start-up, which we would eventually name Uplister Inc.

The ease with which we were able to raise finance for our start-up in that period is in stark contrast to the state of investment capital today. On the West Coast, the levels of investment have declined since 2001. In Europe it has slowed to a dribble. The impact of this new conservatism on innovation is marked. The dizziness of innovative start-ups sprouting new ideas and new versions of new ideas in the period up to the 2001 dot bomb crash was breathtaking. As many others have explored very fully, the fact of the web suddenly made all kinds of things conceivable. As a generation we set about conceiving of all those possibilities. The ideas exploded and were refined, trialled and retrialled. The instant accessibility of the entire consumer base online demanded new offerings, but also made iteration a feasible model of product development. Many of those ideas are still being worked through now commercially and technically, but the flow of genuinely new models and genuine business innovation is definitely slower. There is a more focussed, more business-like energy in the newer start-up communities around the Rivington Streets of London and New York. They are just as passioinate, but suffer less from the headiness of that first phase of internet boom.

Uplister Inc's concept was based on a fundamental realisation, prompted by Napster, that digital distribution would commoditise music. Only a few digital distributors of music would prevail and all the music tracks in the word would be atomised, turned into individual digital downloads to buy. When consumers were spoiled for choice, they would need help discovering new music and in rediscovering old favourites. We returned to the concept of mixtapes and started to focus on the 'playlist'. We predicted that the playlist would be the new unit of music consumption. Previously, the label manufactured and controlled CD determined which tracks would be played, in what order. With all the world's music fragmented into individual tracks, the music industry would need a way to re-bundle, in order to preserve volume and high price points. As our thinking evolved, the best model turned out to be a subscription service, where consumers paid a few dollars a month to access all the music, which had been organised by real music specialists not algorithms.

Once we had a single price point, we added the concept of playlist-sharing, allowing people to find and play each others' collections easily. We enriched the original concept of a playlist from a simple listing to something more narrative and visual, it could contain text and graphics. We encouraged people to tell stories about the music: the history of a band or a genre, why that music was important to that person, or just make a great sequence for a spinning class or a workout. People created their playlists and then uploaded them. We were to provide the music. We called the company Uplister. We had wanted to call it Uplist.com but that had been taken already by a porn site. Our tag line was - Organised Music Anarchy - it seemed to sum up the world we were living in. In some ways it still sums up the online music world.

Leaving EMI was one thing, but getting a visa under the California State quota system was literally a lottery. Even as I applied for my HIB visa in March 2000, the NASDAQ reached its highest ever peak and promptly collapsed. For six agonising weeks until May, I waited for notification while the NASDAQ plummeted, recovered slightly and then continued its inexorable fall. My application was successful and as soon as I got the news, I was able to resign. Outside the corporate constraints of a large multinational, the sense of freedom was intoxicating. For the first time I would go to work in the mornings without a shot of corporate adrenalin in my stomach. Instead of worrying about who was going to stab me in the back, I focussed on how our service could be more attractive to more consumers.

August Capital invested a modest $6m in our company. We starting hiring staff fast, 12 developers in an office in Fremont and the rest of us as business development and sales marketing in a sub-let on Bryant Street in San Francisco. A few months later, we all moved in together to a new space in Oakland and started to get serious. We'd begun by building a desktop application but rapidly moved to deploying a web-based app. The development team worked hard. Our marketing team was working on branding, others were out getting college radio geeks to generate tens of thousands of high quality playlists to suit every taste and activity of human life. Schneider, Taylor and I worked on strategy and licensing. The whole team would go out to sushi karaoke bars, bonding afterwork and playing ball games against other eminent budding dotcoms, including our sister company that was funded by the same VC, Listen.com, which eventually would become the Rhapsody music service.

Two major problems brewed on the horizon. Firstly, the market was beginning to crumble, investors were starting to lose faith in the whole dotcom thing. Investors behave the way any other industry sector does, like sheep. Their first retreat was to move away from business to consumer companies (B2C) and favour business to business (B2B) models. When you're starting a company though, you can not simply change the business model to follow where the funding is going. Although people talk about the skill in choosing when and how to pivot, there is also much to be said for good old fashioned tenacity. The second problem for Uplister was that licensing the music from any of the majors was incredibly difficult. Our model didn't suit their fixed template and just because I had been at EMI didn't do anything except open the door to us a little earlier. Once we got inside, the licensing discussion was like wading through the same swamp all over again. No matter how familiar we could get with their arguments, we couldn't get them to move any faster. We made our repeated visits to EMI in Hollywood, Universal in Santa Monica, to Sony Music on Madison Avenue, Bertelsmann on Time Square and Warner Music in the Rockefeller Centre. Each company representative (and ex-colleague) was courteous, welcoming and demonstrated no interest in issuing licenses to us for less than a million dollars upfront each. We did have that money in the bank, but if we went that route, we would spend all the money we raised in one week. We decided that licensing from the indies would be cheaper and allow us to prove our concept.

Matador Records, TVT Records, Beggars Banquet, Sub-pop were all keen to play ball. We certainly had music to playlist, but our model absolutely required us to have all the music to make it work. The majors wanted to do deals like the one EMI had done with Musicmaker - that was a new benchmark. We simply had to raise more money, but what had earlier in the year been expressed as market concerns, soon enough became downright disenchantment. In the period from

March to August 2000, as the NASDAQ zoomed south, companies like CISCO and Amazon lost over 80% of their value. Other companies like Pets.com went under altogether.

By mid 2001, the investment we had received in 2000 needed supplementing urgently. There was a new reality, the bubble was bursting. In fact as the year went by, bursting was hardly an adequate expression. Cratering was more like it. Our most frequently visited website was Fuckedcompany.com. It relayed in lurid detail, all the gossip about which company was next most likely to become a cloud of dust. At first, the site had been a useful place to figure out which companies might be failing so that other predatory start-ups, who might have been more recently funded, could go after them and poach their good staff. By 2001, it became simply the journal of record of the dot com bust. An entire sector of companies had been part of one great, collective R&D party but now, instead of a sponsored champagne reception, we were enjoying more of a bring-your-own-bottle-and-drown-your-sorrows party.

The Kaiser Building in downtown Oakland, CA. is a large 60's office block with a curved grey anonymous front, facing out over Lake Merritt. In the centre of its atrium, a water feature gushes intermittently. During the summer months, it got switched off because of the energy crisis in California and the threat of rolling black-outs. Most of the responsibility for the erratic power supply was down to poor management by the California power authority, but they blamed the black outs on the practices of a little company in Texas which would become almost as famous as Napster, called Enron.

Uplister's new offices were on the 22nd floor. A more corporate, 'grown-up' space, it contrasted with the funky loft the company had occupied in downtown San Francisco. The more corporate context made the team focus harder on building the business. Declining investor interest, however, was proving a major distraction to the senior management team. We chased the next investment-round persistently, working to keep our conversations fresh with each new potential investor. As we went through this mill, one of the most telling comments, one of them made to us at the conclusion of a particularly tedious conference call, was: "The thing is, you guys are shooting way ahead of the duck". That had been precisely where VCs had wanted to invest previously and no doubt they would return there sometime soon. It was a classic unanswerable comment.

While the investors were using their favourite cliches to suggest we were too early, it is the non-technological entrepreneur's constant concern that the development team are too slow. In their cubicles, the company's engineers continued to work on the next beta-release version of the product. I was trying to accelerate the process, asking colleagues why we could not get an earlier demo out sooner so that we would have something to show when we went to see the next investor. I had to learn that not upsetting developers is critical in these tense periods of small company evolution. Even though the sky may be falling, developers still prefer to live in private worlds, keep their heads down and focus on the code. They want folk like managers to take care of things and not cause any ripples.

Our Senior Software Architect, Eric winced at these precipitous executive urgings. He needed mental and physical release from the strain. His cube was decorated with an assortment of Japanese foodstuffs, Hello Kitty pink cookies, and peppermint peanut bars. It also boasted a working doorbell that rang quietly as if connecting way back somewhere inside a dimly lit mansion. This was how I often felt about Eric's brilliant mind, but we bonded over Napster. His latest download, "Drunk Russians sing the theme from Titanic", blared out into the quiet of the office. The true value of Napster for Eric, was not that it represented "all the world's music for free". What turned him on about Napster was its ability to find novel musical exotica in the midst of all the generic pop pumped out by labels. Napster offered mixes and mash-ups of songs that would never be allowed to be released commercially, like the infamous Eminem / Britney Spears Slim Shady / Oops I did it Again remix or the DJ Dangermouse, Grey Album mashed up from the Beatles' White Album and Dr Dre's Black Album. A combination of label resistence and artists refusals have ensured that neither of those titles was ever officially released. To this day, the only way to acquire the Grey Album is to download it illegally. We were convinced, if only we could create something that put its focus on discovering and surfacing this kind of underground, eclectic content, everyone would love it and no one would sue us. Unfortunately, we also suspected that no investor would fund a project designed to make esoteric mash-ups the centre of attention.

Schneider and I went to visit with the guys at Napster. They had just moved to a warehouse building in Mill Valley. Sean Fanning, the notorious founder of the company, sat in a side-office, baseball cap over his eyes, working on a new project which he refused to discuss. Six months earlier he had appeared on the cover of Time magazine, billed as the man who "upended music". A few weeks earlier we had gathered at the court house in downtown San Francisco to hear the judge of the Ninth Circuit rule in the case brought against Napster by the RIAA. The appeal was against the labels' injunction ordering them to shut down the whole system. Fanning was a folk hero but he seemed remote, uninterested in exploring possible collaborations. He had been paralysed by the law suits. Nothing could be decided until the effect of the injunction was adjudicated. The best days of Napster were already over. Although the appeals and counter pleading continued, Napster eventually succumbed to the legal pressures. It was acquired by the Bertelsman corporate group who allegedly acted preemptively, without consulting with the Bertelsman Music Group at all. The bruising litigation had however damaged the Napster brand forever and despite limping on in various incarnations that still exist, the site never delivered the returns that it so dramatically offered when it first appeared.

At Uplister, we decided to take a leaf from Napster's book and seek an unlicensed source for music - purely for demonstration purposes. We connected Uplister's back-end to the Gnutella peer-to-peer file-sharing network. This was the decentralised network which solved the problem that Napster had of holding all the music on one server. Gnutella went on to become the disruptive power behind Kazaa and Limewire. We created a version of our product that drew down the music files from the network to demonstrate the power of our playlisting capability. We called it Twizzler and we loved it. Suddenly all the text-only playlists that our thousands of users had created, lit up with the audio. We didn't have to limp along with thirty second clips or make playlists only from the music we had licensed. Now all the music for all the playlists we could think of was available - courtesy of the global file-sharing community. Uplister plus Twizzler was an utterly compelling product - and totally illegal. If the battle lines were being drawn up between technology and music, here was a product that made us straddle the lines completely. When music executive talked about crossing to the dark side, this is what they meant.

We took Twizzler to our executive meeting to discuss. On the one hand, we knew that if we put the product out, we would become the new heroes of the burgeoning online music community. We also knew that if we put it out, we would be toast. The labels would sue in a blink of an eye and the venture capitalists would have their best excuse for not getting involved.

Meanwhile, our team watched their managers' every move, our facial expressions before and after every phone-call. They had absolute faith in our ability to pull this thing off and we drew on their energy and commitment. We also had to keep our investor Board Director Andy Rapport on side throughout all of this. He normally came to visit us for Board meetings, this time we needed to go see him for a chat.

Our experience typifies the complex relationship between innovation and investment, and between investors and entrepreneurs. So many content owners will argue that simply because technology is able perform a certain function does not mean it should be allowed to do so. Clearly in the case of nuclear weapons or genetics, the very significant ethical and economic issues which arise from innovative research continue to provide communities with troubling problems. The balance between the greater economic good, the greater cultural benefit and the potential for economic growth through technological innovation can not be struck easily. The dot-com boom was littered with interesting innovations like Uplister that challenged existing models but would cost more in overcoming legacy legal barriers than investors had the stomach to risk. If investment in innovation is about de-risking, it still has to have a visible return. Context is everything, much more is possible in an upwardly trending market than in a downturn.

Sand Hill Road is the Wall Street of venture capitalists. It is home to most of the Californian private equity investors who fund Silicon Valley and its surrounds. From the flashy big name firms like Sequoia Capital, Kleiner Perkins and Benchmark to individual investors, most of the buildings along this semi-rural strip are occupied by the investment community. In 2000, rents on Sand Hill Road in Menlo Park, were reputed to have become the most expensive in the world, higher even than Manhattan or London's Mayfair. Decorated generically by oleander, bougainvillia and eucalyptus trees, Sand Hill Road is low key and unassuming in an essentially Californian way. It could be almost any parkway through suburbia or light industrial business park. Yet each of the players whose offices lined the street, is dedicated to spotting and taking a share in the next Facebook, Linkedin, or Pandora. Some are entrepreneurs turned investors like Marc Andreeson who founded Netscape, others are major name strategic analysts, like Accel or Greylock, they like to place big bets and make big wins. Some are ostentatious, some are low key. August Capital who invested in Uplister is one of the more low profile firms. Its lead investor, David Marquart was a founder investor in Microsoft. August's pockets run deep. They share a building with Benchmark who tend to the louder end of the venture capital community, August is happy to be more of a boutique.

The entrance to August Capital is off a carefully manicured pathway that leads into a country club-like campus. The climate is always a little warmer and a little sunnier down the peninsula than in the fog and cloud of San Francisco as if the sun always shines more favourably on the ingenious capitalist and the very wealthy. Gently curving paths, edged with delicate low flowering bushes are regularly watered by the high-tech irrigation system. Fancy sports cars are parked nonchalantly around outside the tree-shaded modernist clusters of white, low-rise buildings. Inside is like the waiting room for a high class plastic surgeon, the artwork is avant-garde but neutral, there is no music. The waiting area looks out over the controlled wildness of the gardens behind.

Andy Rappaport is an urbane, red-haired technologist who, in his spare time plays with a Sand Hill Road rock band. Occasionally Bill Gates shows up to jam. Inside Rappaport's office, a yellow translucent plastic coffee table dominates the centre of the room, surrounded by two Italian office chairs and a white sofa. Two acoustic guitars stand on either side of his desk which is scrupulously empty. Rappaport sits attentively on the edge of his chair, looking enthusiastically back and forth between Schneider and I as we explain the progress our engineering team has made. We explain the slowness of our music licensing conversations and the temptations of Twizzler. He reassures us that we are on the right track, that we should not deviate from our goal or consider laying staff off because of the dotcom slow down. We discuss the next financing round and he urges us to find that third party investor who would help him justify a follow-on investment. He exudes the kind of confidence that comes of years of seeing the roller coaster ride of investment risk, failure and success. The fact that the economy appears to be in free fall around us seems to barely register on our investors. On the contrary, the advice is clear, keep the pedal to the metal, and continue to get as far down the road as possible as fast as possible.

Venture capital is an enclave where confidence, enthusiasm and success are the language of choice. While other kinds of investor may have counselled caution, venture capitalists were not encouraging restraint. They did not suggest that companies consider battoning down the hatches to find ways of weathering the coming storm. Like others around them, our guys retained a positive certainty, refusing to be shaken by the tumbling NASDAQ. From their perspective, the investment in Uplister had been relatively small. They extended the original $6m with an additional $2m bridge, but the shutters would come down unless we could find that third party endorsement in the form of another investor. They had been relaxed about the investment, the sum involved had been almost like drinks money to them. At the same time, they had in mind that for the price of just one or maybe two bottles of Coke, we might just find a way profitably to disrupt the whole bottling factory.

When the finance gets tight, entrepreneurs get inventive. They also hit the road. A trip to New York was rapidly planned to follow up on some of our other investor possibilities. The East coast investment community with its focus on publishing and rights ownership might look more sympathetically on a company that was finding new value in music content. We flew Jet Blue with a momentary sense of celebrating some new efficiency. They definitely had the lowest fares around. No food served on the flights, but there was Direct TV by satellite all the way.

The lobby of North Wit Sound had glass bricks, a picturesque receptionist behind a pale beech curved desk and an Andy Warhol print of Chairman Mao on the wall. Susan Sarodnik was a previous contact of mine. She had been at Bertelsmann when I had been at EMI. She had agreed to take a meeting, but it lasted less time than she kept us waiting in the lobby. Sarodnik was not trying to be rude. She was just a New Yorker and her portfolio of companies was subsiding beneath her feet. The phrasing of the rejection was fairly straightforward. We were "music" and we were "consumer". She said she didn't need to know anything more about us. The firm has simply taken the final step of pulling the plug on consumer. Susan's words reflected the massive withdrawal of investors following the dramatic NASDAQ crash. According to Price Waterhouse Coopers, total annual venture capital investment in the US dropped from $98bn in 2000, to $37bn in 2001, to $20bn in 2002. Sarodnik was patient, enunciated slowly but looked like she was just waiting to clear her own desk.

Outside the late summer sun lengthened the shadows as swarms of office workers strolled across Union Square. Suddenly, we felt like real aliens. As if somehow the start-up excitement and exhilaration had been turned inside out. The constant rejection was demoralising. We felt like social outcasts in our quest for funding, risk-taking pariahs who could not be considered worthy to hang out with solid, salaried, corporate workers. It was exhausting, physically and mentally. The more we saw what whas happening in the market, the more we were convinced that success might be less in financial terms, more in lessons learned and experience derived. Trying to sound optimistic over and over again was tough. But, led on by Toni Schneider's irrepressibly positive outlook, we just got on with giving the best demonstrations of our business we could. New York's speed and energy can lift you and wear you down in a day. We flew back to San Francisco quietly considering our next move. Should we flout the law and launch Twizzler on the world? After all what did we have to lose?

A week later, back among the cubes and diligence of Oakland, I received an unexpected phone call from the RIAA requesting my presence in New York once again. I was to be deposed by Michael Robertson's defence lawyers in the Universal vs Mp3.com law suit. Mp3.com went public on July 21, 1999 and raised over $370 million. Its success was heralded as the way forward for indie musicians to avoid the major label trap. But Robertson continued to try to extend the functionality of the site to make it more user friendly. He added a new feature called MyMp3.com that allowed consumers who had bought a CD and uploaded it to a digital locker to then stream that music over the internet to whereever they happened to be, to their preferred device for playback. This is a service which today is offered by Apple, Amazon and Google. But Michael Robertson was on the RIAA watch list and as soon as the new service appeared Universal Music Group sued. The case had been rumbling on. It would eventually be settled and Michael would be forced to pay over $50m to Universal. At Uplister, we were horrified by the distraction that this represented. I was also concerned about the viewpoint I would be expected to uphold. I am sure that Robertson had me deposed because he knew I'd left EMI and had moved across to his way of thinking, but I was still bound by contractual obligations to the company. Clause 7.8 of my contract clearly set out "Surviving rights and obligations". For the purposes of a depostion, I was still under EMI ownership.

One more thing would make the next couple of days interesting. A digital media, cloud storage company called Loudeye was going public. I met them a few months before I left EMI and sensed they might be interested in hiring me. We were friendly but never did a transaction. I was surprised to receive a share offer under their "friends and family" scheme. My wife and I discussed it and decided that we would, for the first and only time risk some investment in this company at its IPO. There was no conflict of interest. I was always careful to stay away from any personal financial involvement in the deals at EMI. This time, I felt entirely justified in taking part. The IPO was on the day of my deposition.

The RIAA were in control and the briefing was intense. A deposition can last from six to twelve hours. Witnesses should be prepared to be present and available for that duration. The defence deposition in this case, would be unlikely to have a very clear line of questioning. The aim will be for them to listen out for a slip up or a hint of something which might serve to undermine the prosecution argument that the MyMp3.com service was a breach of copyright. Answers should be kept to a minimum. No elaboration was required unless requested. It is quite permissible to encounter a memory lapse, in which case simply say: " I cannot remember". Do not try to make any jokes or be humorous in any way at all. Do not enter into any kind of pleasantries with prosecuting counsel either during, before or after the deposition. Remember he is not to be trusted.

The IPO was one of the holy grails of the Internet bubble. Even when the gold-mine was caving in all sides, there were still companies trying to go public. Loudeye Inc was one of the last to get itself even a fleetingly breathtaking valuation. In the bubble, the art of IPO trading was to "flip" your stock, cashing out at the moment you judged the market to have reached a reasonable peak. In another aspect of how the internet created a new sense of a level playing field, inexperienced, day traders across the US were treating the NASDAQ like it was Vegas.

With a popular IPO, the volume of trading could be immense, the value of shares highly volatile during the day. At the height of the madness, a stock on first offering might go out with a first asking price of $10 or $12 and then rise on the froth of the market to several hundreds before falling back for reasons having nothing to do with the commercial performance of the company. Eventually the stock would slide back to a "reality" which might still massively over-value the company. By the end of the bubble, a highly rated company called ArtistDirect Inc went public and enjoyed the dubious distinction of being the first music stock to drop below its own IPO offer price before the end of its first day trading. The dot bomb did not eliminate this practice. Investors often have larger appetites than they do memories. Facebook is a more recent example of a tech stock going public to much excitement followed by inevitable disappointment. The effect is to leave shareholders (including employees) with stocks under water which is demotivating to staff and puts a great deal of Boardroom pressure on the company.

I sat in the deposition meeting room at the end of a long table. On my left, sat six lawyers from the RIAA, on my right, five prosecuting on behalf of Michael Robertson and Mp3.com. At the far end of the table, the video camera perched on a tripod, next to it a stenographer with a transcription machine with long keys just like in US courtroom dramas. The interrogating lawyer stalked around, consulting notes, sniffing the air and casting side-long glances. The first wireless device capable of relaying real-time stock prices to hungry investors had just become available (a Palm VII). It was a must-have for any self-respecting member of the digerati. One of my lawyers had his and couldn't resist occasionally taking it out to check the NASDAQ. As I was being pressed by the attorney to give my views on personal copying, the Loudeye IPO was taking place just down the street and my wife back in California was handling the transaction.

The questions began and I answered in the requisite monotone. As an ex-employee of a major record label responsible for internet music deals and for setting internet music policy for the company, the questions were about my personal music technology habits. Had I ever copied a CD across to Mp3? How might I go about doing that? Do consumers have a fair usage right to copy CDs? They wanted me to make an error, reveal an inconsistency that could be used to point to some personal departure from the rigid corporate party-line. The fact that I no longer personally supported the label's viewpoint simply added to the stilted nature of the conversation. I toed the line I no longer believed in. Even after I had left, the company still had a hold over me. It was not a proud moment.

Finally, lunch-time came and we paused. The operator switched off the video camera and everyone pushed back their chairs, stretching with relief from the mixture of tension and tedium. Our senior lawyer checked his Palm VII again. Then, in front of everyone, I completely let down my guard and asked him how the Loudeye IPO was going. The Mp3.com attorney turned sharply and looked at me . He made a note on his yellow legal pad. My stomach lurched. No one said a word. My lawyer looked at me blankly and we left the conference room without another word. Outside, the lawyers simply ignored what had happened and gave me feedback on my performance. Silence seemed to be the best policy. As soon as we had a lull in the conversation, I borrowed a mobile to call my wife. She informed me that it was all completed. The stock had risen well, she had sold out near the peak and we had made a few thousand dollars. She sounded giddy with excitement. I felt nauseous and miserable.

We resumed and the prosecuting lawyer pitched straight in by asking if I was currently an investor in or owned any shares in a digital music company other than the one I worked for. I had just sold. I was not a shareholder. If he had phrased it differently and asked me the question to include past ownership I would have had to disclose my Loudeye investment. He would have pursued that for all it was worth. Although, I had no reason to be nervous, the deposition environment is harsh and unremitting. Defence lawyers are trained to provoke guilt or suspicion among the innocent. I had no conflict of interest. I did not abuse my position, but immediately was put on the defensive. While the legal arguments provoked intellectual interest, the tactics of litigation seemed manipulative and sordid. The last thing I needed was a summons as a witness in the main trial. However ambivalent I was about the arguments in this case, I was glad not to have opened a chink of opportunity for the lawyers. I didn't have time to get caught up in the arguments about some one else's innovative investment, I had to focus on mine. Uplister needed all its team on-side.

After the lawsuit, a financially weakened Mp3.com was acquired by Vivendi Universal for approximately $372 million. Vivendi did not continue the MyMp3.com part of the service and had difficulties growing. Eventually they dismantled the site and sold the assets to CNET in 2003 who, in turn were acquired in

2008 by CBS. Mp3.com now redirects its traffic to sister company, Last FM.

After the excitement of New York, the ensuing weeks back in San Francisco returned to their regular pattern. At the beginning of August, the lease was up on my family's rented house in the hills of Berkeley. We decided that my wife and the kids should go back to London where they could start in English schools in September 2001. I flew back to help them settle into our London home and see if I could create UK opportunities for Uplister, important UK indie labels showed interest. Beggars Banquet were keen to get involved. They introduced us to Channel 4 TV who loved it and wanted to create a Chart Show based on the most popular playlists on our site. The pace in the UK seemed much slower than in California. Decisions were not being made. Interested English folk who would think hard were not what we needed. We needed decisive customers or investors who would be bold in the face of a dwindling market. Those were becoming rare beasts on either side of the Atlantic.

I returned to San Francisco and moved into a friend's apartment temporarily. With these few prospective London deals in our pocket, our existing licenses and Twizzler up our sleeves, maybe some merger conversations could be worth exploring. In the next building to us in Oakland was a team who called themselves Savage Beast. The company had built a music recommendation engine based on the classification of tracks by volunteer musicians. The CEO was Tim Westergren and we arranged to meet in his office. When we got there, we didn't know whether to laugh or cry. Unlike us, Tim had not heeded the words of his VCs and he had stripped the company down to Marie Celeste mode (named after the famous ghost ship which had no visible crew). He had no staff except for his two co-founders and they had moved back to LA to live at home. None of them had been paid for six months, but they were determined to hang in there. Westergren and his team had no idea how they would get themselves out of the mess they were in, but his determination and self-sacrifice were outstanding. We wished each other well out there, but concluded that there was not much to gain from merging our businesses. We parted amicably into the evening and counted ourselves lucky that we had at least been able to pay our staff for all this time. Two years later, as the markets recovered, Westergren got new backers, changed the name of his company to Pandora and opened for business not as a recommendation engine but as a streaming music service, using his engine to drive the playlist. In 2011, he took his company to the NASDAQ in an IPO which was regarded as the most successful since the first bubble.

We continued to plan and plot. We explored with August how to make our cash last longer. We talked again about how to use Twizzler to best effect. The entire team continued at full throttle on our mission until the evening of September 10th, when we all finished work and went home as normal.

At 6am the next morning, the world changed before our eyes. I woke to the screams and terror of my host family as they watched what was happening in New York city, relayed live on TV. For a couple of days none of us could move. Quite literally, I could not fly home. The streets were eerily quiet. We crept around in a state of heightened anxiety, anticipating another attack. I managed to confirm a seat on the second flight out of San Francisco for London that Friday. That was probably the worst flight I have ever experienced, the JetBlue shuttle seemed like another world. I didn't return to the Bay Area until the Autumn of 2003 when I was CEO of Sibelius Software. We wound up the affairs of Uplister shortly afterwards. Somehow in the traumatic days after 9/11, the backups that should have kept the Uplister code and database secure, failed. When it came to shut down, there wasn't even an asset left to sell on for a few pennies to some other torch-bearer. In some ways, I felt better for that and it made little difference to the investors.

Our investment in the importance of playlists had its payoffs. Many of the ideas that we created for Uplister found their way into other services. iTunes regularly features artists' playlists on its front pages. LastFM and Spotify allow the easy sharing of playlists between listeners. Numerous companies have appeared since Uplister who have seen the importance of playlist culture and carried it forward. Our sister company Listen (also funded by August Capital), changed its name to Rhapsody, a US subscription service which recently acquired the commercial incarnation of Napster. Tim Westergen's Pandora is one of the leading music services in the US. At the time of writing, it has still not succeeded in negotiating licenses to launch its service in Europe. Westergen still challenges the labels' license rates set for streaming music. My partner Toni Schneider went on to run a webmail company called Oddpost which he sold to Yahoo. He is now the CEO of a company called Automattic whose leading product is the world's most-used blogging platform Wordpress and is on the Board of BandCamp one of the most popular platforms for artists and bands who want to release their music without the help of a label.

4. Emotional corporations

As a general rule in business, declaring war on a very large proportion of your most committed customers is not recommended. Yet, through its anger and frustration at technological change and by sheer litigious aggression, that is exactly what the music industry did. During the period from 2003 to 2009, the music industry initiated over 30,000 lawsuits against music fans in the US alone, citing copyright infringement on peer-to-peer networks. They called it Operation Hubcap. The name possibly derived from the idea that they were targetting "street kids" who also participated in the hip-hop-inspired fashion of stealing hubcaps from parked cars and automobile brand-insignia like VW signs. Operation Hubcap targets included children, students, the elderly and the recently deceased. The aim was to put people off file-sharing. As an education program it certainly had some impact. The effect was to drive an immense wedge between the labels and music fans. It created a rift which has not been repaired. It heightened exactly the wrong kind of bad-boy image for the major labels. This was no cool, aggressive street boy stance, this was harsh impersonal, corporate aggression and it alienated a generation of customers who, with equal disdain, the labels called "freetards".

From 9/11 onwards, the music industry placed the phenomenon of file-sharing centre stage, as the single greatest challenge to its business model. The controversy sparked by Napster, and carried forward by numerous other services like Kazaa, Grokster, Limewire, and Bit Torrent highlights a simple technological fact. If music can be played back via digital technology then it can be copied and shared over the internet. Since the very earliest days of clips of music being made available on FTP sites and accessed by Fetch, the writing had been on the wall. The response of the music industry to its increasing unsexiness was to place the blame on what it called "piracy". While pirates were traditionally shady characters with home duplication machines, selling rogue CDs in the streets of Bangkok, the internet globalised their business.

Suing pirate sites was expensive and seemed to be a game of wack-a-mole, hit one site and another one popped up the next day. The industry's frustration with file-sharing only grew as it seemed that the technologists were playing cat and mouse with rights owners. A shift of tactics was required. So, Hubcap was rolled out and for the first time, inspired by the RIAA and reinforced by the BPI and IFPI in Europe, the music industry started to sue its own fans. A more effective negative public relations campaign could not have been orchestrated.

It is simplistic to argue that file-sharing is the root cause of all the economic problems in the music business and that remains the industry's lobbying refrain. Recorded music's consumer "share of wallet" declined significantly in the 21st century. The overall size of the business diminished by approximately 30% from what turned out to be its all-time, CD-fuelled high in 2000 of approximately $30bn (global trade revenues per annum as set out by IFPI - International Federation of Phonographic Industries). While some of those losses may well have been attributable to file-sharing, other growth sectors have created a new highly inter-connected consumer technology landscape which has simply taken away consumer-spending from recorded music by making more compelling offers. Major social media activities, games industry growth and mobile phone adoption have all grown at the expense of music, both in terms of spending and attention. Whereas teenagers used to spend time just listening to music on CD, cassette, radio or TV, there are now many more calls on their time. Spending hours on Facebook or Twitter has reduced the amount of time traditionally high spending youth devote to recorded music. The growth of console, online and mobile gaming since 2000 also led to that diminution.

The frustrating irony for record companies, however, is that despite these competitive threats to music's "wallet share", and even as file-sharing has grown, so has the overall consumption of music in general. Consumers have shifted from purchases of new music to purchases of tickets to see music played live. The incredible success of iPods and smart-phones has meant that more people than ever have returned to listen again to music that they may have purchased years earlier. This is a major cultural change from which recorded music has yet to recover.

The way in which digital music has been presented and sold online has suffered a failure of the imagination. Music's sense of excitement and creativity has been lost and I blame iTunes. Vinyl LPs were at the heart of an experience which was broader than just the music itself. A band's mystique was to be found like ancient markings, in the graphics, the design, the sleeve-notes, words etched into the inner-grooves of the vinyl or what might be heard if the record were played backwards. A sense of romantic intrigue about the message a band was conveying or conspiracy theories about an artist could be imagined (or carefully planted) in the paraphernalia of the old music formats. At times the mystique even extended into the dingy vibe of indie music retail itself. Labels started to have memory lapses about how to weave this magic when they rushed to re-issue their catalogue on CD and sell it in supermarkets. When they moved to digital and online retail, their recall appears to have failed completely. Despite all the underground and alternative culture that the online world first possessed, it became mainstream very rapidly and lost its ethos in the process. Today if you buy an album on iTunes, it is almost impossible to find out the names of the musicians performing, let alone what instruments they're playing, who produced the album or where it had been recorded. A lack of respect for the musicianship and the craft of music-making has accompanied the hasty bulk uploading of music to the commercial web. The details of who played what and where were the train-spotterish, geeky things that got hardcore fans excited - and hardcore fans were the ones who spread the word to the rest of us. We have lost much of this and not yet learned how to revive it online, yet it's all there to be reinvented in digital form.

Operation Hubcap highlighted an identity problem for labels which has still not been resolved. What should the relationship between a label and its customers look like and, indeed, who are the labels' customers? While the lawyers prepared their law suits, label sales staff busily tried to reassure failing music retailers that these aggressive market tactics would drive fans back into their bricks and mortar stores. Meanwhile, marketing and A&R departments began slowly to understand that they might need to cultivate a new kind of direct relationships with fans. They might need to understand the patterns and trends in musical tastes at a consumer level if they were going have any chance to influence them. One message was clear: the band is the brand. Labels should be invisible marketing hands in this, just like advertising agencies sit behind general consumer brands. The problem came when the labels attacked fans in the courts and tried to control the way the music could be consumed. The fiercely manipulative aspect of their relationship surfaced. It gave the fans increased justification to go file-sharing, particularly since artists were so ambivalent about the commercial probity of their own record labels.

Direct engagement with a band live is the opposite of the impersonal, manufactured experience of buying their music.

The visceral, ephemeral nature of a live gig has greater social resonance today than rushing off to download a new single - although it may be that watching a much talked about new video on Youtube is beginning to reappropriate some of that excitement. The shift in public interest to live music was certainly part of a desire for a more authentic experience. "I was there when Ray Davies turned up to play with Mumford & Sons at the Apollo Hammersmith theatre or when Iggy Pop dived half naked into the audience at the Cambridge Corn Exchange". These fan experiences are exclusive, one-off's shared only by those in the room. If suing their fans confirmed one thing, it was that there is a relationship between record labels and fans, but it is a bitter one. A much more genuine and rewarding relationship exists directly between artists and their fans.

Mainstream adoption of new technologies also, surprisingly, led to an increase in their rejection. In the 90s, the cliche was the kid who knew how to programme the video recorder better than the parent. In the new millennium, the grasp of technology was widespread. The cliches are that to be "tech savvy" is the norm and our children are "digital natives". The consequence is that we expect young consumers to be able to use file-sharing clients, hack games consoles, and prefer YouTube to MTV. It turned out that they also want to have real, live music experiences, go to festivals, sleep under canvas, revive the banjo as a lead instrument, eat organic food bought from independent suppliers and ride bikes rather than drive cars. Festival organisers responded with enthusiasm. Events like Loolapalooza and Glastonbury were already well established, but around them mushroomed dozens of new festivals across Europe and the US. Mintel reported that between 2005 and 2010, sales of tickets to music festivals increased by nearly 70%. In the face of this kind of surging shift to live, record companies tried to get involved by demanding a share in artists' touring revenues. Such efforts were not well received. In October 2007, Madonna announced a new recording and live performance deal, not with a record company but with Live Nation, a live concert promotions company.

Consumer pressure on the labels grew as their attempts to assert tight control over their product continued to fail in the marketplace. Despite the labels' efforts, music retail was suffering, badly. In December 2006, the last Tower Records store in New York City closed its doors. The idea that digital rights management (DRM) or technical protection measures could stop consumers copying music and therefore drive them back to retail was clearly not working. A change of stance was required. DRM clearly now stood for Doesn't Really Matter. Label executives gradually came to realise that the technological inevitability of file-sharing did not have to mean that fans would not pay for music at all or that the entire model was lost. It required a painless and convenient experience, not one fraught with artificial inconveniences. Piracy and consumer file-sharing were going to be a constant reality, alongside which they would have to learn how to grow a legitimate digital music market. They just needed encouraging in some new ways. In February 2007, Apple's CEO, Steve Jobs, published an open letter calling on the "big four" music companies to sell their music without DRM. The following month, EMI took a lead amongst the majors announcing that it would abandon technical protection measures for tracks it released on iTunes. It took another two years, before the other majors all reluctantly followed suit. Books, movies and TV shows on iTunes are all still hampered by DRM.

Later, in October of 2007, the English rock band, Radiohead directly engaged the market reality that payment was merely optional. Free of their record contract with EMI, the band released their In Rainbows album on a "pay what you think it's worth" basis. With this move, they garnered worldwide acclaim and publicity for placing their fans at the heart of a new "trust-based" economic model. The band were already massive and had established themselves as a global brand through over a decade of touring and marketing investment by EMI. The model worked. Although they have not revealed precise figures, analysts have determined that the band would have made substantially more from In Rainbows released on trust, than they would via a label release. The experiment's success encouraged further innovation. It did not solve the problems for fledgling bands trying to find their way through the market to visibility without the help of a major label, but it paved the way for further evolution of models. Without In Rainbows, we would not have the pay-what-you-want or contribute what you like models of companies like Kickstarter and PledgeMusic today, which ask fans to contribute in advance to help the band produce a project without the need to sign a record contract with a label.

*

In 1969, Elizabeth Kubler Ross wrote a famous text called On Death and Dying. In it she described five stages of grieving which she had identified through many years of working with the bereaved, particularly children. Despite their self-professed ruthlessness and business objectivity, I have observed that the behaviour of the major record companies in response to the changes forced upon them by the internet closely resembles the five stages of grief as described by Kubler Ross.

The five stages are:

Denial "this can't be happening to me, none of this stuff is important. No licenses needed."

Anger "why is this happening? Who can I blame? Who can I sue?"

Bargaining "make this not happen and in return I will take control of things myself"

Depression "I'm too sad to do anything, the end is nigh, it's all gloom, doom and piracy"

Acceptance "I'm at peace with what happened and we're working in a new era."

During the decade of 1995 to 2005, the major record companies would prominently display each of these behaviors,

Denial in the context of the music industry took the form of ignoring the most innovative and progressive developments, even when they came knocking on the door. In 1997, MP3.com was launched. In 1998, the first MP3 player, the Diamond Rio was launched, and 1999 was the year in which the infamous Napster was unleashed upon the world. Each of these products and services sought to obtain licenses from the major labels. At one point or other in their development, it became clear to their owners that they would be able to provide online distribution and retail for digital music. Application to the major labels for such licenses in such circumstances is far from automatic. As part of my role in all this, I witnessed the indignant denial of licenses except on terms so outrageously rapacious as to render business models non-viable.

Licensing of digital rights for downloading or streaming, for bundling, for subscription or for sale is a complex business. Services wishing to offer a comprehensive range of music need to obtain licenses from all the majors and the independent labels. They also have to obtain licenses from the music publishers too. In Europe, that could mean trying to obtain over 30 separate licenses. For this reason, the Pandora interactive music service does still not operate in Europe. The first sign of being in denial - not even considering that new services were licensable.

The second stage of grief is anger. In the music industry, anger nearly always takes the form of litigation. In 1998 the RIAA unsuccessfully sued the makers of the Diamond Rio MP3 player. In 2000, Universal Music Group successfully sued MP3.com for breach of copyright. Also in 2000, A&M Records successfully sued Napster for creating an infringing service. Then in 2003, they turned their anger on consumer and launched 30,000 individually targeted lawsuits at music fans. Later their ire shifted to the file-sharing websites.

In 2005, the RIAA sued Kazaa (and MGM Studios sued Grokster). In 2006, they commenced proceedings against Limewire and in 2008, the Pirate Bay was the target of litigation. Internet Service Providers were not neglected either, the BPI and Tiscali famously fell out in 2008. While the failed attempts to introduce the US SOPA and SOCA bills into Congress combined with the successful if botched passing of the UK's Digital Economy Act were the occasion for numerous, near litigious angry exchanges.

The third stage, bargaining, was also a significant stage in the cycle. In the music industry, bargaining means letting the music company attempt to take control by acquiring small challenger tech companies. In 2001, Universal Music Group successfully acquired MP3.com for $272m. The following year, in 2002, the Bertelsmann Music Group acquired Napster for $85m. Subsequently in their conversations and settlement attempts with both Kazaa and the Pirate Bay, licenses apparently were offered in exchange for a willingness to cease and desist.

Legalized, licensed versions of Kazaa and Napster did briefly surface, but neither failed to gain any commercial traction - not least because they had established such deep brand identities as free services that charging for their offering just didn't seem to fit. Bargaining for the music industry, meant negotiating with the technology by attempting to do for themselves what the disruptive new entrants had sought to do before they were stopped by litigation.

Like night following day, depression followed much of this aggressive behavior as digital sales continued to stutter along and nowhere near act as a replacement for the rapidly declining physical sales. Throughout this period when the physical sales model was dying, all the other parts of the music ecology were changing in relation to it too. Live sales increased, a sense of artist empowerment grew. Record label executives talked about the depressed music market, but it was of course only a depressed recorded music market. Other parts of music seemed to be be doing better.

The cycle has repeated itself several times: head in the sand denial, followed by angry litigation, followed by acquisitions of innovative businesses, bargaining to do it all themselves, followed by a depressing subsidence of sales and eventually we have recently started to see a degree of acceptance and moving on. There are now plenty of signs of acceptance inside recorded music companies, but it is also clearly a generational matter. Older executives wishing to cruise to retirement are less interested in reform than the new generation who not only know the internet but are hungry to exploit its immense potential.

What is curious about this is that companies are traditionally managed to be rational and objective. Management business objectives are supposed to be impersonal. There is little room for emotion - except of the right variety - positive passion is now allowed, but other emotions from the great spectrum of human feelings are not welcome or appreciated. Businesses are designed with resilience, double-blind checks built in to mitigate against any dangerous, emotional vicissitudes of individual employees. Major national and international institutions create MBA courses which preach a doctrine of calculating, dispassionate objectivism in business strategy.

Over-achieving CEOs are respected for their hard nosed approach, their refusal to be distracted or swayed by any softness in targeting their business objectives. Soft numbers are disdained, hard facts are highly valued. In complex, large-scale corporations, layers of management structure are templated and reproduced in different territories, across different cultures. Companies do everything they can to reduce the effect of national characteristics. Difference is eroded and even as more enlightened perspectives have sought to reduce sexism, racism and ageism in the workplace, this has only served to further the demands of objectification of business challenge and enterprise solution.

Just as individual humans respond to the loss of a loved one, in the traceable ways mapped so insightfully by Kubler Ross, so large businesses seem to respond to the loss of a business model in a very similar, very human manner. I would not try to make an excessively literal application of these responses, but it is surprising to find the correlation at all. From 1993 to 1995, a state of denial seems to most closely describe the behavior of record companies in the face of the collision of the internet and mp3s.

The labels pretended that the Internet was irrelevant, they ignored those who advocated it and sought to retain control over their businesses in the traditional ways they always had. As it became more difficult, the responses of the industry as a whole displayed classic symptoms of grief. Why this occurred here and whether it is true also for other industries is harder to unpick.

Certainly there are those that would point to this as demonstration of the essential organic nature of human cultures and societies. The behavior of individuals in the organism is compounded into the whole. While each individual may perform a different task or function, the manner of behavior and the mode of interaction with others as they relate to each other and to competitors creates team culture. For the most part, because of the bullish, target driven, objectivism inherent in many business approaches, the culture of large corporations in particular has tended towards the emotionally illiterate. Whether the lack of women in the Board room and at senior executive levels has added to that is worth exploring. Certainly, it is widely recognized that successful women in the workplace tend to achieve their goals by being more masculine in mode and by playing down their gender. Alternatively, the other stereotype sees women ruthlessly exploiting their sexuality to gain advantage in the workplace. Either way, there is a correlation it seems to me between an emotionally illiterate work-force and the behavior of a corporation as a whole or indeed an entire industry.

Kevin Kelly, the internet pioneer, has recently argued that technology effectively moves as an organism. He sees a kind of collective unconscious at work which exists over and above the competing efforts of individual companies to create this kind of global progression. Technology's openness and accessibility means that once a development has occurred in one place on the globe, then it has effectively occurred everywhere. Kelly suggests that some innate drives in particular technological directions such as increasing speed of processing power or a drive towards sharing and collaboration are collectively induced not objectively directed.

Not unlike early ecology movement theories about the earth as a single organism (Gaia) these ideas originate from the same kinds of observation, I've made here. Whether consciously or unconsciously, the industry displayed very human characteristics in grieving at the death of its own business model.

Each time that I've talked about this, I've felt an overwhelming sense of both the comic absurdity of this idea and also a slightly unnerving feeling that it has some substance. Researchers with more time and a wider purview than me could look into this in more detail with more examples from other sectors and find other contexts of industrial change to see if there's anything it it, whether it is unique to the creative industries or visible in other sectors, whether it is only found in the context of technology driven systemic change or whether or kinds of transitions induce similar responses. I don't know the answers to any of these questions, but it would be interesting to know whether creative companies alone behave with such innate humanity.

In the case of music, there is also another argument that might be made which suggests that the "industry" responded emotionally to its circumstances because it is so small and its major companies act closely together, so frequently. The number of individuals involved in making strategic decisions about the launch of such initiatives as Operation Hubcap was in effect so small as to provide none of the insulation from emotion that larger scale corporations build in.

I don't believe that the music industry is unique in this. Companies that deal in creative work and creative artists as their "suppliers" are more likely to be able to act with a degree of emotional understanding than those which don't. Certainly it is the experience of most people working inside music companies that the relationship with artists is often a paradoxical one. Artists are both respected and despised. They are respected because the closer you get to the creative process the more its complexities and challenges become apparent.

The role of A&R staff (like editors in publishing houses, or dealers in contemporary art) is about building trusting relationships with signed artists. The A&R has to encourage and point to commercially fruitful musical directions as well as be critical and ultimately strong enough to reject a piece of work. That kind of relationship is very private and very public at the same time. The A&R is the first champion of a piece of music even before it leaves the studio. They are also the custodians of whatever secrets or inconvenient truths may be associated with the creation of the work.

All of this implies a degree of empathy and a degree of passionate involvement in an artist's or a band's work. It also implies a degree of cold hearted commercial perspective. None of this seems to imply emotional illiteracy. It would all suggest a deeply felt involvement in the creative process and its commercial development. In the end, that commitment and passion are the emotions which justifiably provoke the anger and outrage in the face of unauthorized file-sharing and we will see in the next chapter the way in which artists do feel a great deal of conflict in these circumstances.

Yet, A&R is just one part of a music company's make-up. Its sales, marketing, distribution and legal departments are all equally key to the success of a label. Somewhere in those areas, one might have hoped that a sense of a relationship with a community of music fans might also have registered. Someone somewhere might have paused for thought and pondered what it would do to the relationship with the paying public if they started to sue them Instead we saw a combined singleness of mind which while it may have contained a few individual voices of dissent, from the outside certainly looked and sounded fearsomely categorical in its pronouncements with the results we have all seen.

After twenty years of music online, acceptance is finally arriving and there is a new hunger to embrace almost every new technological innovation with music, before any other form of content can get to it. The music industry is more optimistic and more outward facing now than it has been for a long time. Whether its executives are any more emotionally literate than they were previously, remains to be seen.

5. CONFLICTED CREATORS

As economic influence has shifted from recorded to live performance, so artists themselves become more and more central to how money is made in the music industry. Yet, making a living as a band has become harder and harder. The number of bands out there trying to make it has grown substantially as the internet has lowered the barriers to self promotion and marketing. Youtube is the best breeding ground for young unsigned bands in the world and lots of artists are starting to build audiences well before they sign to a label - if indeed they ever do.

Once they enter the label world though, all the structures and processes of the business still tend to favour labels over artists. Labels write the artists' recording contracts not the other way around and they are still notoriously opaque. Offering contracts that still commonly contain clauses to compensate the label, for example, for breakages and expensive packaging, in a digital age betrays a backward looking approach. Sales of recorded music in the UK are still divided 65% physical CD and vinyl compared to 35% digital download or streaming. But breakage of CDs is a much rarer occurrence than was the case when the industry depended on delicate old vinyl. The fact that vinyl still sells in small numbers to DJs and aficionados is not really justification for retaining vinyl-related language in new recording contracts. Of course there are lots of new kinds of deal being created. Independent production deals, production and distribution licenses, digital only deals and increasingly various versions of the so-called 360 deal which seeks to grab a piece of the full range of rights and revenues that an artist might expect to generate. Labels are signing fewer acts and while the live scene is good for the established artist, touring can still be very expensive for a new band.

In the face of all this, a group of artist managers in London, in mid 2008, began to argue that, if only they were better organised, then they should be better able to control their own destinies, as the transition to a fully digital business continued. The industry was not well structured for the online era, a new organisation was needed to help speed up the change, change the architecture of the industry and ensure a better deal for artists in the process.

The Featured Artists Coalition (FAC) was organised by a group of managers from the Music Manager Forum (MMF) led by Jaz Summers, a veteran manager of Soul II Soul, The Verve and Snow Patrol, Peter Jenner, Pink Floyd's first manager, David Enthoven and Tim Clerk who managed Robbie Williams and Brian Message one of Radiohead's management team. Summers with his old fashioned mixture of charm and thuggery, persuaded one of the industry collecting societies, Phonographic Performance Limited (PPL), to lend the FAC some money to get started. The FAC was all about giving a voice to artists and their subscriptions would serve to fund some staff and repay the debt. On the Board were Annie Lennox, Nick Mason (Pink Floyd), Dave Rowntree (Blur), Ed O'Brien (Radiohead), Billy Bragg, Sandie Shaw, Howard Jones, Robbie Williams and numerous other luminaries.

I became the first (part-time) CEO of the Featured Artists Coalition when it launched in March 2009. The organisation wanted a seat at the industry negotiating table. It didn't necessarily know what it wanted to negotiate exactly but conversations began quickly with pillars of the recorded and live music establishment; the PPL (how is the debt that the FAC launched with going to be repaid?), BPI (what can be done to make artists' contracts fairer?), and the Musicians' Union (how are these two organisations different from one another?). Merely announcing the existence of an organisation does not lead to its acceptance. The labels' initial welcome quickly muted as it became clear that the FAC would be critical of the music industry status quo. Welcome shifted to outright opposition, as the artists decided to make themselves more visible to politicians and government officials in order to address high level changes in the Digital Economy Act legislation that were being pushed very rapidly through committee stages at the time. The UK was also in the grip of a General Election campaign that would see the Gordon Brown administration shunted aside by the new Tory-led coalition of Cameron and Clegg. In circumstances like these, politicians adored nothing more than to be photographed in a mutual love-fest next to cheeky pop celebrities.

The flashpoint came around file-sharing. The UK's media and technology industries were convulsed throughout 2009 by the intense debate surrounding the draft legislation which would become the Digital Economy Act. The draft contained measures intended to curtail file-sharing, much of which reflected the most aggressive positioning of the major labels. Some of the language appeared to have even been drafted by the BPI. It imposed new responsibilities and costs upon companies that operated broadband networks and internet service providers. The proposals included measures to block consumer access to websites which might be inciting copyright infringement and the disconnection of the personal, domestic internet feeds of individuals who were perceived to be file-sharing excessively. This type of particularly troublesome consumer became the beneficiary of their own category name. Coined by a highly regarded British civil servant who privately confessed to me that he wished take the opportunity to "revivify the English language", these large-scale file-sharers became known as "egregious offenders". Given the degree to which internet access was now regarded as a human right, fierce arguments broke out over the technical definition of "egregious" and precisely how such individuals might be identified. Advanced technical investigation methods were proposed such as "deep-package inspection" and other forms of interception, including the reading of email and other internet traffic. Many argued these measures were likely to compromise both personal privacy and freedom of speech. They raised concerns over freedom of speech and human rights which remain if anything more critical today as more and more public services become dependent on internet delivery.

Recording artists are more conflicted about file-sharing than almost any other topic. On the one hand, they see it as theft of their creative work by the very people, their fans, who ought to value it the most and therefore pay for it. On the other hand, the whole reason that they make music is because they want to share it and file-sharing online is today's most natural, effective way of doing that. In many respects, once an artist or a band start to be the subject of file-sharing, it is now recognised as an achievement, an accomplishment of a certain degree of visibility and success. However ironic it may be, the active engagement with an artist's music by large numbers of file-sharers is an indicator of demand. The nature of the conflict became very intense. The media were quick to seize on the new organisation as pitching itself aggressively against the labels. Some of the higher profile Board members of the FAC gave national press interviews that presented the sense of conflict they felt in terms that suggested that they were not opposed to file-sharing. Even as they tried to point out the inescapable reality of file-sharing in the day to day nature of available technology and consumer behaviour, the media were quick to characterise their comments as a pitched battle between major named artists and their record companies.

The labels responded with fury, urgently trying to suppress the heretical voice of this new industry body that seemed to threaten them. They mobilised some of their more willing artists. Lilly Allen and Elton John both came out aggressively criticising music fans who file-shared. The topic raged in the press and media and, of course online. Universal Music allegedly brought in their public relations guru, Matthew Freud, to draft blog posts for Lilly Allen in which she appeared to lambast fans who file shared. At one point, Lucien Grainge who runs Universal Music worldwide, allegedly referred to the FAC as the "Taliban". Perhaps such conflict was inevitable given the mixed feelings of everyone involved. At the FAC, I tried to advocate a progressive and pragmatic view. I tried to encourage artists to acknowledge technological inevitability and at the same time to explore ways of creating better consumer experiences that would increase value and the willingness to pay. In some ways, the artist community inevitably played a naive game against a knowing and calculating industry that was carefully positioning its arguments to win shrewdly thought-through strategic, lobbying goals. Artists are very good at saying what they believe. The more passionately they believe something, the easier they find it to talk about. Being tactical and manoeuvring for media positioning is not something that comes easily to most musicians.

File-sharing appeared to be dividing the artist community, ironically just as the FAC had been set up to try to unite it. We organised a private, artists-only evening meeting at Air Studios, a beautiful recording studio, housed in an enormous old church in Hampstead, north London, and owned at the time by George Martin (producer of the Beatles). There was an incredible turn-out of artists. Members from all sorts of bands showed up including Pink Floyd, Radiohead, Blur, Travis, Keane, and Marillion. Individual artists present also included, Billy Bragg impassioned and politically savvy, David Arnold composer of the Bond music, talented indie artist Patrick Woolf, and Mike (the Wombles) Batt - in this context something of a ringer as he was both an artist and vice-chairman of the BPI. In an upstairs mastering suite, where he was working on a new record, George Michael had a runner provide him with reports of the proceedings. Annie Lennox had her digital representative relaying events by phone. Meanwhile, no one quite knew how to interpret Chris Martin of Coldplay, who sent his apologies. I had the dubious honour of chairing the meeting. It felt a bit like a cross between a historic parliamentary occasion, an alcoholics anonymous meeting and a music industry awards show. Fifteen minutes after the discussion began, with suitable drama, an uncharacteristically timid Lily Allen came into the room, clutching a glass of red wine and crouching behind the back row. As she was recognised, she was encouraged forward, applauded for attending and quickly found a seat in the front to take part in the debate.

Lilly was in equal turns tearful, angry, eloquent and foul-mouthed. The whole debate didn't entirely revolve around her, but she and Billy Bragg became the respective voices of the opposing positions. Lilly vehemently condemning file-sharers, Billy robustly defending their freedoms. The arguments swung back and forth. The conservative view is as strong among many artists as is the more liberal position. For an hour the debate went on, artists taking turn to state and restate the positions. They glared at each other across the room. Crispin Hunt, a member of a band called the Long Pigs, got very angry. He got up indignantly, shouting: "I can't understand why you're being so soft on them. They need to be told what they're doing is wrong", and walked out of the meeting (he subsequently became very active in the FAC and joined its Board). Billy Bragg, ever a "voice of the people", delivered a rousing speech about needing to nurture fans and how the relationship an artist has with his or her fans is the only one that counts, how punishing listeners could not be the solution. Half the audience applauded wildly. The other half scowled.

As the clock reached 9 pm and the debate kept on going, I thought maybe a vote might be a way to achieve some closure. I felt pretty certain that they would not agree on the key issue of whether or not to support the suspension of "egregious offenders" internet accounts. The positions just seemed too far apart. Maybe we could come out of this with some compromise, perhaps they might agree on something about pushing cultural change and encouraging new business models. Perhaps they could conclude by emphasising the positive stuff they did all share. I tried to herd the cats. Then something remarkable happened. As I pushed them to close, they wanted to argue on, the energy in the room suddenly lifted. Ed O'Brien from Radiohead suggested that perhaps not complete suspension, but restrictive bandwidth slowing could be a solution. The ability to use email and basic web-serving could be preserved as a human right, but the high bandwidth needed to make file-sharing worthwhile could be reduced.

The room leapt excitedly on the compromise. Billy Bragg stood on a chair and started trying out the precise language of a press release or perhaps it was a proclamation. Patrick Wolfe who has never been pictured smiling was laughing. No matter that the proposal would cost more than cutting people off. No matter that people could still file-share, but just more slowly. No matter that squeezing bandwidth might require as much of an invasion of privacy as its complete suspension. A compromise position was visible and the community of artists always shy of confrontation, leapt on it. The artist community had become united. Euphoria was in the air. Lilly and Billy hugged. A common perception of artists as a community capable of empowering one another has been rare in the music industry. Very few occasions arise or are created when whole communities of artists get together. Their commercial circumstances more often than not pit them in rarely spoken competition with each other.

The effect of this event was to reposition the FAC as an organisation capable of assimilating the different views of all its members. But aside from the day of its launch, there's not been another occasion of such drama. The FAC continues its work but has yet to succeed in making itself into the influential force to which it aspires. Despite their unpopularity with consumers, the labels still exert a disproportionate political influence as they find common cause with movie studios and book publishers. What some have called "lobbynomics" combined with the commercial pressure they could apply to key artists voices would always make it difficult for challengers to be heard. The Air Studios meeting ended with a feverish capturing of this compromise, written out by hand on a long scroll of paper by Billy Bragg and Fran Healey lead singer in the band, Travis. In the end though, artists were still left, having more in common than they realised with the reporters huddled in the cold outside, waiting to capture their statement.

Not long after that meeting, I stood down as CEO. The role of the artist is more central to the business than ever and the Board rightly wanted the CEO position filled by an artist. Unfortunately, it is easier to talk about an artist community than to build one. Artists are individualistic mavericks. Team players in bands but as eccentric as they have to be. The market rewards talent in a wider variety of ways today than ever before. Revenues generated from an artist's career have shifted away from a simple majority of earnings derived from recordings and everything else being icing on the cake, towards a much more complicated mixtures of different revenue streams, live, sync, recordings, licensing, video ad revenue, sponsorship. Each of these revenue streams may complement the other or massively outstrip everything else. The band's value as a brand, is best derived from a dextrous and individual playing to the strengths of an artist in each of those different areas. Some bands are more about live than recorded music, some never perform but license lots of music to film, tv and commercials. Some bands are all about making great videos. Increasingly it seems likely that bands will be able to make money out of advertising revenue on YouTube channels, alongside revenues from streaming audio services like Deezer and Spotify. Songwriters and composers of course sit at one remove from live performing artists but in many ways share in this new diffuse economic environment. It remains incredibly hard to make a living as a musician and the competition is intense. The number of global super-stars will only reduce in this environment and even the new pop heroes promoted out of TV talent shows tend to be national rather than international celebrities.

The fact is that musical raw material in the form of a willing band has never been in short supply, despite the fact that real talent is still a rare and fantastic thing. The highly competitive nature of the market makes it very difficult for artists to have any strength in contract negotiations with major media companies. There are always more artists wanting a record contract than being offered one and this does not make for a strong negotiating position. Whether it is a record label or a brand sponsor, there is an imbalance of power. Traditionally, in the pre-internet world this meant that artists signed deals that offered a sizeable cash advance but usually left them massively un-recouped and no longer in possession of their own copyrights in their own material.

Worse than this, the way in which managers in the music industry are remunerated tends not to help developing bands. Artists' managers usually take around 15-20% of an artist's revenues. The result of this is that some of them have a tendency to look for deals that will pay out significant advances. Once a deal is signed, the danger is that these managers are likely to be incentivised to think more about their next big payout, rather than the campaign of promotion and marketing that will lead to recoupment of their already signed artists. I'm not suggesting that managers are not interested in making their artists successful, after all their reputations as managers depend on it. Sadly though, the likelihood of an artist succeeding is low - the average ratio at a label is traditionally about 10% of signings become hits. The effect of this is to make many managers of newly signed artists or as yet unsigned artists very keen to maintain good label relations. It is only the more powerful managers who are like to question the system; managers whose artists have acquired a degree of independence from their label or who have at least achieved a level of success whereby there is some mutual interdependence.

Fortunately, the levelling of the playing field brought by the internet and the various platform opportunities to reach consumers directly, has changed the position somewhat. Artists may have some new, less punitive routes to market, but they are for the most part not much better off because of the massive price erosion that has occurred in recorded music.

Open access websites like the internet underground music archive (IUMA) and Michael Robertson's mp3.com started a train rolling that would not stop. Artists were increasingly doing it for themselves. The internet lowered the barriers to entry but raised the noise level of artists competing for attention. One off projects like Radiohead's In Rainbows, and other projects from artists like Trent Reznor of Nine Inch Nails offered music to fans for whatever price they wanted to pay or let them interact with their work by remixing it. As more artists demonstrated a willingness to experiment, so more entrepreneurs and new businesses popped up trying to make commercial sense of the ideas. Big name bands who were free of their contracts, were the ones who could experiment. New young acts, with no name to speak of, would have to try much more innovative models to catch attention - or use really cool effects to make themselves audible about the noise.

New music fans are choosing to spend their money on different kinds of return. They are not just interested in passive consumption, but in buying into and getting involved in someone else's passion. The ultimate extension of this is the companies who now offer the services of bands to come and play mini-gigs in private homes. The growing popularity of this kind of return to something like the salon culture of the nineteenth century is another way for artists to begin to establish themselves. Word of mouth from these sorts of private, exclusive events can lead slowly to larger audience and larger venues. Music fans are cultural consumers who value authenticity and personal interaction alongside a purely material return. By attending live shows and contributing to someone's new project, a generation of internet users have indicated a preference for credibility and participation over what looks like corporate endorsement and exploitation. Marxist academics still find it stylish to refer to Napster as having "liberated the creativity of the multitude from the servitude of capitalist exploitation." This seems so shockingly wrong as not to be worth arguing, but it is still picturesquely repeated by some Professors of Cultural Studies on the conference circuit. The search for a new business model for music and arts content clearly does not revolve around an arid, purely financial transaction, but it does still require some transaction. It's just that, for this new generation of users, it must involve some kind of sustaining interaction too. What music fans will and won't pay for is getting clearer even as it continues to evolve. It's about a set of cultural values that are developing and emerging as more important than a set of economic models that focus on mere technicalities like price-sensitivity or elasticity.

As the major labels with their studio stars shrunk in number, increasing numbers of musicians started casting around for investment from new sources. Fans and supporters were an obvious source. Quirky English progressive rock band, Marillion, were one of the earliest proponents of this approach. In early 2000, they sent a mail shot to their hardcore fans to invite them to pay £16 each to subscribe to an album before it was recorded. The response was enormous. Over 12,000 fans responded. The band was able to make the album on the back of this fund-raising effort and released the record the following year with the names of all the contributing fans printed on the artwork as a reward. In touching tribute to their fanbase, the album was called Anoraknophobia. The band members all featured in promo shots wearing anoraks. Mark Kelly, the band's keyboard player and main songwriter became the first artist CEO of the Featured Artists Coalition and also the first performing artist to sit on the Board of the UK collecting society, the PPL The DIY movement has grown rapidly, but it's still a gamble for a new artist with no profile.

The problem of getting noticed and building a fanbase remains for new young acts. Radiohead, Trent Reznor, Marillion could perform interesting experiments which helped break the mould, but their innovation was dependent on the fact that they already had large, loyal fanbases which in each case had been built by big budget, major label marketing campaigns when they had been signed. Once they had been dropped from a label or had escaped from their contract, then they were able to capitalise on their band as brand. For new artists, trying to get noticed without big budget backing requires a completely new set of tools. The key to building fans today is still through performing shows, but also through releasing music for free, making videos for YouTube that for some reason get a lot of attention and promoting all of the above through Facebook, Twitter and any other available form of social media.

A cluster of new companies has emerged who are in business to help this process. Companies like Musicglue (of which - full disclosure - I am Chairman), TopSpin, and Bandcamp all provide free or low cost platforms that allow bands to sell music, tickets and merchandise directly to their fans. Some also provide tools or services that bands can buy to help promote themselves or create marketing campaigns. Bandcamp now boasts over half a million registered bands and has paid out over $23 million to artists. According to Toni Schneider who advises Bandcamp, most bands set a minimum price for their music or merchandise and then let fans name their own price above that. Across the entire site, the average name-your-price ends up 50% above asking. Some fans will pay $100 for an album just because they love the band so much. Albums outsell tracks 5 to 1 on Bandcamp. Meanwhile Musicglue has now distinguised itself by developing an easy to use platform that allows bands to sell tickets, music, merchandise and other digital assets in any bundle, with any form of discount they choose. Its simplicity and easy of use certainly seems to indicate an important direction of travel in making this kind of service accessible.

Marillion drew upon their fan community to pre-order their work as a series of one-off, web-based interactions. Kickstarter and PledgeMusic are large-scale platforms that allow hundreds or thousands of projects to advertise themselves to fans and enable donations at an early stage in production or even at concept stage. Musician, Amanda Palmer, gained considerable attention by being the first artist to raise over $1 million in donations (actually $1,192,793) on Kickstarter for her new project combining an album, artbook and tour. She had set her target at $100,000. The exuberance of videos, the inventiveness of offers that go with each level of donation are key to the excitement that Kickstarter creates. It's not just "please buy my music". Kickstarter and Pledgemusic create new windows on what's in production now or on what's possible. It gives new a kind of transparency that invites a plethora of different ways to participate in artists' projects or indeed in re-issue or catalogue projects. How sustainable it is, remains to be seen. There is already the kind of noise of an exotic bazar on these platforms, where every price can be negotiated, but you can never be too sure of the quality. This is the "post-Napster" generation in action. Alongside funding platforms like Kickstarter and Pledgemusic, there is a whole generation of companies emerging to serve bands across a very diverse range of areas from mobile apps, to ticket sales, to insight and analysis drawn from social media activities, to simple hosting of music, to enabling bands to set up an entire virtual label and release interactive music projects using 3D technology and augmented reality.

6. Tarzan economics

While culture and history make progress at their own leisurely pace, technology has sprinted ahead. The web has engendered feelings of liberation to a generation. We share a new belief about what the world could become, not just aided by technology but transformed by it. It is no longer rhetoric to say that the internet can bring freedom and democracy. Many of us have come to believe that, through the web's openness, we can both transform existing businesses and create completely new ones. The web itself, of course, has developed and changed. The web today includes the mobile web and a hybrid mixture of new devices accessing it. Keeping the new web open and maintaining its level playing field is a major ongoing challenge in its own right. There are plenty of politicians, major telecommunications companies and large media interests who are keen to reduce the openness of the web, precisely because a closed environment would allow them to maintain a version of their business model, less radically transformed. It's easy to understand why. The pain involved in that transformation lasted much longer and was much greater than anyone ever expected. As each stage of this journey unfolded, the effects of corporate grief at the passing of a business model became more visible, in both its early denial and its later litigious anger. I have to confess that I always believed a point would come when the degree of commercial pain would simply be too great to bear and that radical change would, therefore, have to come about. I was mistaken.

The power of current shareholder sentiment should never be under-estimated. Financial markets demand quarterly reports to demonstrate the health of the companies in which they are invested. Share prices need to be continually buoyed up by near-term anticipation. Analysts may ascribe some value to long term strategy, but they will always take greater account of the bottom line in the current quarter. The task of building a new high-risk, unproven technology-dependent business, at the same time as sustaining an old established but dwindling, box-shifting business, is a challenge greater than most companies could face down. This is the riskiness of what is called Tarzan economics - a term which I believe may have been coined by the Washington DC-based, music technology activist, Jim Griffin.

As companies struggle through the jungle of doing business on the web, they swing from vine to vine, from business model to business model. To succeed, they have to learn how to grasp a completely new vine ahead of them while still holding on to the old one that sustained them previously. If the new vine turns out to be weak - the business model unsustainable - it will come away in their hand. If they've already let the old one go too, the company falls to the ground. Plus, of course, it's very hard to make progress, swinging through the jungle if you're clinging on to two vines. Music on the web has offered so many different strands to grasp at in the form of new business models. Very few of them have looked strong enough to clutch at - even if the companies proposing them were cash rich enough to yield a fat license fee.

The struggles of the major record companies are very similar to those of major newsprint publishers, book publishers and film studios. None of them has found an easy path through the web to change, although others have had the chance to learn from music's mistakes. It may just be that the fundamentals of Western public stock-markets are simply incapable of managing the massive degrees of disruption provoked by the web. The markets themselves have been seduced repeatedly by the web. They attribute staggeringly high valuations to Google, Apple, Amazon and latterly Facebook. Despite growing legal and ethical concerns about their behaviours, a glaring disjuncture has emerged between the valuations of those trying to migrate from analogue to digital and those companies who have been internet businesses from the beginning.

Apple's share price reflects the immense success of its model. Despite being widely reviled by developers as a poor piece of software, iTunes remains at the heart of the best integration yet of hardware and software for the consumption of music, movies, TV shows and books. Yet, despite Jobs' exhortation to the majors to remove technical protection measures from their music, he stealthily planted his own controls around the borders of his orchard. Its walled-garden may be a delightful place in which to roam, but Apple's ecosystem is still very closed. Moving music off iTunes is still almost impossible except by burning a CD which seems positively anachronistic in today's market. Now the competition is lining up. Challengers in the space are looming, with Samsung using Google's more open Android platform and Amazon demonstrating increasing sophistication in its devices. Microsoft too has demonstrated a tenacity in relation to music, launching a music service on their highly successful X-Box platform, demonstrating a continued interest in music that would not have anticipated based on the sad fate of their Zune music player.

While iTunes represents 85% of today's digital marketplace, in the next twenty years, they are unlikely to retain that supremacy. Music may well, once again, find itself used as a loss leader in the pursuit of differentiation and dominance in new online markets. For the majors, the concern remains that sales of digital music are still not growing sufficiently in value to replace lost CD sales and balance corporate books. Cost cutting and efficiencies can only preserve a model for so long. New services are proliferating, but price points are not rising. The concept of Tarzan economics suggests continuous change, but in many ways the labels are facing a single fundamental challenge which is centred on the viability of their rights model. Spencer Hyman was COO of LastFM when it sold in May 2007 to CBS for $280m. He puts the conundrum very simply: the traditional music business model had three core components; control the means of manufacture and distribution; control the promotion of music to radio, and control exclusive licensing. The worldwide web broke all three.

The web is a copying machine. It breaches copyright like you and I breathe. The fundamental way it works is through a process of caching. Content from one part of the web is copied or mirrored on servers on another part of the web so that content can be more rapidly accessed and the burden on the network reduced. That is the fundamental premise of the entire internet. In the face of this, the record labels' struggle to retain control of their media has been a battle to enforce the most basic elements of copyright. Most people still agree with the need to maintain the fundamentals of copyright law - the right of an author to attribution and remuneration for his or her creative work. Yet anyone with a rudimentary understanding of technology will also understand that enforcing this through the right to prevent others making a copy is now an anachronism so acute as to threaten the credibility of the law.

There is however almost zero political appetite to embrace real reform either in the UK, in Europe or the US. The wholesale redefinition of what constitutes copyright is long overdue because of the evident technical impossibility of enforcing a copy right. Instead though, nations horse-trade on exceptions to the law to allow those with particular needs, such as educators or researchers, to avoid the stringencies of the law or to grudgingly let in one more consumer freedom which only recognises what has been mass behaviour for years. At the same time, rights holders have successfully lobbied to extend the term of copyright's duration in a way which is fuelled not by the public interest but by commercial exigencies as Professor Lawrence "Larry" Lessig, a law reformer from Harvard University, has observed repeatedly in his work.

There have been more reviews of intellectual property law and copyright in the UK, Europe and the US in the last 25 years than in the previous 300 with Banks, Gowers and Hargreaves in the UK, the Australian Attorney-General, the US Copyright Office, all pointing to the problems caused by disruptive technology and making proposals for change. In the hallowed circles of the creative industries however, even questioning the fundamentals of copyright and proposing to replace them with something contemporary and more fit for purpose is seen as tantamount to heresy among rights owners and remains an aspiration at which no politician has even looked twice. Each review has made recommendations that acknowledge the scale of the challenge but has left governments with the politically toxic concept of taking steps that might lead to the dismantling of the legal and commercial basis for the entire entertainment and publishing industry in order to facilitate a future web-based business model that looks scarily unknown and high risk. Tarzan politics is even more unattractive than Tarzan economics.

The web demands a new way of thinking about how to make content accessible. In 2001, Larry Lessig and a group of colleagues proposed their concept of Creative Commons (CC). It is a system for licensing content for non-commercial use. It is based completely on copyright. CC became hugely successful, particularly with web publishers, but in a fashion that was almost entirely non-revenue generating. By 2008, some 130 million items of content had been published under a CC licence. For incumbent copyright businesses, CC looked like a sophisticated attack on the very principles of copyright itself, especially when Lessig was perceived to receive funding from Google. The conspiracy theories abounded. Yet the whole basis of Creative Commons is that it reinforces the fundamentals of copyright while removing for non-commercial users, barriers to licensing that commercial transactions require. Entertainment industry lawyers fought back hard and CC made little impact on formal legislation, but it has been successful in placing a new emphasis on commercial licensing.

Licensing is a philosophy not unlike prostitution. It states that you can use a set of rights for a particular purpose on payment, but you never own those rights and you can only use them in the particular way agreed in your license. The functions that people want to license music for are all approximately the same, but there is a limited supply of music, each track is unique and the choice of which track to use is a very personal choice. The music publishing side of the industry, which trades in the rights to compositions and lyrics, has always understood this. The "sync" market that licenses songs to films, TV and advertising tends to operate in a very handmade way, one song at a time with many individual permissions required from publishers, sub-publishers, and occasionally even from creators. The recorded music side traditionally regarded licensing as minor ancillary revenue but as CD sales have declined, "sync" has grown as a revenue stream. Most of the big money to be made in licensing recorded music, however has been of entire catalogues to consumer music video, download or streaming services. Interestingly though, many of the file-sharing, copyright infringement cases brought against consumers by record companies were based on the fact (little understood by consumers) that when a CD was sold to a consumer, the music on it was not sold but licensed. There is unreadable rubric around the rim of a CD that explains this in opaque, legalistic language.

It seeks to prevent such matters as private copying, still not legal in the UK, and other things like for example preventing a consumer from creating their own radio station and broadcasting the music on the disc or indeed making a file available for others to share.

Licensing individual rights has come under scrutiny but even more so has the other key industry practice of collective licensing. Large and wealthy organisations such as ASCAP, BMI and the Harry Fox Agency in the US, PPL and PRS in the UK have become establishment pillars of the music industry by collecting royalties for performing rights and distributing them to labels, publishers, artists and composers. One of the most intense arguments within rights-owning companies triggered by the web, has been what sorts of rights to grant the collective licensing bodies and which sorts to retain.

As economic pressure has grown, major music publishers and record companies have progressively withdrawn rights from the collective licensing bodies in the US and the UK. Their actions are driven by their desire to control licensing activity in a fragmenting market, to reduce the overhead paid out to the collecting societies, and to gain a competitive edge over the other majors. As the number of majors consolidates, the relative convenience and one-stop value of the large collecting societies has declined. Unfortunately, the effect of undermining these pillars of the industry is to lessen the ability of individual song-writers, composers and performers to get paid at well-negotiated rates. The leverage of the collecting societies to negotiate is diminished, the fewer rights they have to directly administer and the more they become mere administrators of the publishers' deals.

As the slow explosion of music on the web persists, a new architecture is urgently required that is fit for purpose and can suit the needs of the many individual rights owners as well as the large players. Collective licensing has to be the only sensible way forward for an industry whose key assets are millions of fragmented shards of rights, but the mechanism for delivering it needs completely reinventing. Projects such as the European Global Repertoire database, I believe, are destined to struggle. Sisyphus-Like, they are seeking to clean the legacy of dirty data without redesigning the engines that continue to produce more dirt. Instead, what is needed are new digital rights registries and online rights exchanges which register new work only. If the legacy issues of old dirty data were separated from the opportunities in online licensing, then innovation might enable exciting new ways of remunerating creators and rights holders. We have to draw a line in the sand and acknowledge that the murkiness of poor data relating to the legacy of music should not be allowed to contaminate a more simplifed and efficient digital future. Currently the industry is still trying to renovate its old structures rather than innovating entire new processes.

These two large areas of concern are related but separate. The future of how legislation handles copyright in the age of digital reproduction and the future nature of digital content licensing. Fundamental change will in due course be addressed, but we may have to wait many years before the market failure is so acute as to demand it or for the moderately progressive forces of organic change to catch up. Subsidiary to this are more specific issues about commercial licensing at both business to business and consumer levels. The long standing tradition among content creators of the signing of separate rights to separate companies in order to divide and rule needs urgent review. The analogue profit motive that split up rights seems to be counterproductive in the digital environment. If the full range of rights were more commonly bundled together for licensing purposes then the current degrees of friction would be considerably reduced.   This could be achieved by legislative reform and but it could happen more quickly through simple changes in commercial practice. The same question we have encountered before recurs here. How much pain does the industry need to incur before it will change? How far does decline in value of the old model have to go in the face of corrosive technological disruption, before an entire industry realises what is needed to reform?

It is not progress to continually seek to control the reproduction right only to have it slip through the fingers like sand. Creative industry would be much better served by laws which could protect creators and rights holders by acknowledging that uncontrolled reproduction is inevitable as soon as a work is released. To do this requires companies and creators to be able to think about how to manage the very central concepts of copyright in the context of the internet. This requires a legal and a cultural recognition of the essential reality that despite all the wack-a-mole efforts of litigious rights owners, once a single recording has been released in digital media format onto the internet, it is effectively universally available to those that wish to make the effort to find it. The scale of inevitable disruption caused by the internet as the world's largest copying-machine is such that the underlying framework of the law needs to be changed now. Sadly, the vociferous and recidivist efforts of lobbyists to shore up their position has made it difficult to enable constructive public discussion of new ideas in this field. Creative industries need to find new ways to preserve the fundamentals, the remuneration of creators, ensuring they retain attribution of their work and how to ensure that they determine a degree of integrity in their work.

Some might argue that the success of new services like Spotify and Deezer represents sufficient economic benefit to the rights owners that changing the fundamentals would be an unnecessary and over-ambitious task. Personally, I believe that the law needs to be in step with reality, not behind it. This is not an attack on the fundamentals of copyright at all. On the contrary, it is a recognition that it is so important that we need to make it relevant again to culture, society and the economy.

By way of solutions to this degree of fundamental problem, an economic argument has developed around how to monetise the amount of creative work being shared on the internet. In 2009, the IFPI published its Digital Music Report in which it claimed: "...the music sector is still overshadowed by the huge amount of unlicensed music distributed online. Collating separate studies in 16 countries over a three-year period, IFPI estimates over 40 billion files were illegally file-shared in 2008, giving a piracy rate of around 95 per cent." By 2012, it estimated that 3.6 billion downloads were purchased globally in 2011, an annual increase of 17 percent (combining singles and album downloads). At the same time it reported that "28 per cent of internet users globally access unauthorised services on a monthly basis and that 60 per cent of e-book downloads in Germany are illegal, according to Börsenverein des Deutschen Buchhandels, the organisation representing German publishers and booksellers". It is very hard to disentangle the facts from these kinds of statistics. The degree of unauthorised file-sharing does not have a direct correlation to the lost paid transactions. Nor is it clear what proportion of files downloaded could be attributed respectively to music, ebooks, movies, games, pornography or undesirable, subversive material like bomb-making kits or civil disobedience plans.

In 2013, Spotify and data analytics company Musicmetric (where, interest declared, I am Executive Chairman) made a study of bit-torrent filesharing activities in the Netherlands. Two interesting insights emerged from the work. One is that file-sharing is not a constant activity, but one

138

that is divided between a small hard core and a much larger long tail of users. That long tail of users display remarkable variation and infrequency in their usage. The total number of hardcore file-sharers in the Netherlands turned out to be relatively small 250,000 or so. There was a much larger number of irregular users but they were much less frequent and churned regularly. The research also identified that the arrival of Spotify as a legal service coincided with a marked cessation of the steady growth in file-sharing that the territory had seen previously.

The reality is that file-sharing is a given. It will continue and if it is pursued by the legal measures rights holders propose, it is likely to move underground and become less detectable. As I write, the use of virtual private networks to mask file-sharing activities is increasing as are other IP-masking methods of avoiding legal scrutiny. The opportunity to monetise this activity is there. If the efforts of rights-holders continues to push this activity underground and into dark-nets, then any opportunity that there might be to monetise it, will be diminished - possibly even be permanently removed.

Once entrepreneurs understand that the clash of technology and content is based on conflicting business models then possible solutions start to emerge. Internet service providers are happy enough to sell subscriptions to consumers when the consumption of bandwidth only increases as creative work is shared - legally or illegally - they don't really care. Bandwidth providers and Google simply want to give the consumer a faster more efficient service so long as it drives easily manageable flows of traffic across networks and eyeballs to advertisements. The fundamentals of the problem have remained unchanged since the internet became business viable. Content companies sell their products in a manner that is barely changed from the way they did in the physical world. Selling units not access to music flies in the face of eat-as-much-as-you-like broadband subscriptions. That's why access models like Spotify and Deezer are starting to look more attractive, although they still only represent less than 10% of total music industry revenues. Both companies have achieved bundled licensing arrangements with mobile network operators where the revenue models are much better aligned. The mobile operator can offer a differentiating benefit to its subscribers and the use of streaming music across the service, complements by simply increasing the end-users consumption levels of the host service. The nature of mobile networks makes them more discrete environments than the broadband internet thus allowing these kinds of deals to be implemented more easily. In theory, there is no reason why such a service could not be established over the entire internet to cover all the music or indeed all the digital content that is being consumed.

Some have argued that the imaginative licensing of more innovative services will be a better means of reducing so-called "piracy" than the game of litigation that creative companies have pursued to date. Understandably, rights owners are pursuing both strategies, but many argue that they have been slow to license new legal services. As described earlier, the music majors charge high advances for access to their catalogues and the level of control and ownership that they seek to exert over those services can inhibit growth. When challenged, IFPI often mentions that there are now many more licensed services than ever and that the number is growing globally. They tend not to mention how many of those are lookalike straight download retail stores with very small customer-bases which do not thrive in the face of the major players. iTunes for downloads and Spotify for streaming, still represent 85% of digital revenues globally. Observers await with interest to see whether Apple will establish a streaming subscription service to compete with Spotify. Its radio service is a step in that direction and will compete with other existing major services in the US like Pandora and I Heart Radio. The more innovative the service, the less likely it is to find it easy to get a licence. Innovative services might seek to enable mash-ups of tracks, or they might associate a song with imagery or product advertising that might be disapproved of by the artist, or a new service might cannibalise the fragile sales of existing services.

The degree to which rights owners take an ownership piece of a service also affects inevitably the degree to which they will license a competing service. At first, as I recounted, the attitude was to take an ownership piece of everything. While that was not the case with Apple's iTunes, because they simply could not get there, Spotify is 18.5% owned by the record labels. In December 2012, Warner Music-owner Len Blavatnik invested $130m (£81m) in subscription streaming service Deezer, apparently making him a "cornerstone" investor in the business although still not a majority shareholder. His investment vehicle Access Industries also subsequently invested in the new Beats Network service which was due to launch late 2013. These kinds of investment do indicate a vestigial desire to regain control of the means of distribution of content. They can also affect the ability of competing services to obtain licenses. It may be mere coincidence that Bloom.FM a new streaming music service for mobile, financed by an anonymous Russian investor, has not at the time of writing succeeded in securing a license for music from Warner Music Group despite obtaining licenses from the three other majors.

As the provider of an innovative service offering, as I discovered at Uplister, the question has inevitably been: do I try to modify my service to fit into existing license terms or do I create what I think is the best possible service for consumer and then try to persuade rights holders to give me a license for it?

In response to this high degree of friction in licensing, the UK Hargreaves Review of Intellectual Property made a strong case for a Digital Copyright Exchange, an automated licensing environment. Hargreaves argued in broad terms that if licensing could be made more automatic more frequently, then more projects would get licensed and therefore more revenues would be generated. Others have countered this by arguing that large-scale licenses for new services demand individual negotiation because of their innovative nature and that of course the individually negotiated licences were of considerably greater value than those issued under standard license terms. The debate around this has been vigorous but often confused. The issues surrounding the one-off licensing of individual rights for individual usage such as sync licensing of a song to a TV drama soundtrack is a totally different matter from the full-catalogue licensing requirements of consumer music services. Both would benefit from less friction and a reduction in the number of individual licenses required to be negotiated, but the mechanisms and the parties involved can be quite different. This area is very technical and has become so complex and the public arguments so very often confused and at cross-purposes that the industry has not achieved any focus that would induce any real appetite for more rapid levels of change from within.

The simplistic ideas that reducing online "piracy" to nil would solve the problem is still the predominant view heavily argued by content companies. They argue that all this reform of licensing talk is well and good but it is distraction from the main problem. Hence Operation Hubcap and the ongoing lobbying efforts of the music industry trade associations. Copyright law is one of the places where what Professor Ian Hargreaves calls "lobbynomics" triumphs. The degree of focus on "anti-piracy" activities and legislation is out of all proportion to other issues in the creative industries. Recent unpublished work looking at the strategic objectives of the main UK public sector organisations funding the creative industries, revealed over a dozen different strategic objectives. These included access to finance, skills, entrepreneurship, international export and inward investment, adjusting imbalances between major urban conurbations and outlying regions, and reform of the intellectual property framework. Most of these kinds of policy priority are intended to benefit a range of types of companies from start-up, to early stage and all kinds of other businesses. Only a few big changes will be of benefit to larger corporates. A recent UK Parliamentary Culture, Media and Sport Committee enquiry into Support for the Creative Industries focussed almost entirely on the issue of internet piracy and took no interest at all in those other areas of policy initiatives that are also designed to support creative industries. They are not alone in their apparent myopia.

There is little sign of fundamental reform visible anywhere around the globe. Instead, lookalike legislation has been proposed in many countries to address rights owners' anti-piracy agenda. In the UK, the Digital Economy Act (2010) was passed hurriedly into law at the dog-end of the Gordon Brown Labour Administration. Over the subsequent three years, it has endured a troubled implementation largely due to the lack of clarity in the drafting and insufficient debate before it was passed into law. In the US, the recent SOPA and PIPA legislative initiatives only served to deepen the rift between technology companies and content businesses. Both sides blamed each other (and the power of each others' lobbying) when it ultimately failed to pass into law.

I believe fundamental reform is required and alongside it a radical alignment of the interests of network operators and content service providers. The law on copyright needs to change fundamentally and globally, not at the edges but at core, to preserve the basic tenets and incentivisation of creativity. The new environment of the internet requires a new reading of copyright. The speed of technological change will continue to highlight the anachronistic nature of existing statutes. If culture moves more slowly than technology, then the movement of the law is often barely visible to the naked eye. Most of the incremental shifts to liberalise copyright are through the creation of increasing numbers of exemptions to copyright. The net effect of this is simply to add complexity. As some point, such complexity becomes counter-productive. Arguably, it already benefits only the lawyers who battle to draft and then interpret the legislation. Joseph Tainter's 1988 work The Collapse of Complex Societies provides a theoretical scenario which is relevant here. When the complexity of the law is so great that even lawyers cannot explain it, then consumers gain their own license to behave badly and no amount of education will fix it.

The radical change involves finding another way of addressing the problem by exploring how to take into account and monetise all of the transactions across the internet whether legal or not. The trouble is, radical transformation of networks into intelligent networks, content aware, consumer aware networks offers both major commercial advantages and significant moral hazards. This is not a new idea and it has been argued for in a variety of flavours, but it has the fundamental merit of seeking to align the commercial interests of the internet service providers and the content creators. Both Spotify and Deezer have gained rapid traction in the market place through doing deals to bundle their service with mobile operators. This is an incomplete step in that direction. Doing this across the open internet is a slightly different challenge, although increasingly the difference between mobile internet and the connected one will reduce.

If the activities across an entire network were to be monitored and monetised comprehensively, we would see greater efficiencies in transactions and a greater ability to manage major consumer concerns of trust and privacy. The monitoring of networks by police and security agencies is already greater than is broadly recognised. Recent revelations regarding the US security services Prism system have revealed that the measures to be vigilant against terrorist activities, hard-core pornography and other criminal behaviour have intensified considerably beyond most consumer expectations. The threats of cyber-crime and military-style cyber interventions are increasing daily. Equally, it would seem that encroachments on civil liberties and privacy are growing in frequency too. Just as the military encouraged the creation of the internet in the first place and academics saw its wider application, so we should track how the technology is being developed and try to seek the most beneficial societal and commercial outcomes possible. The advertising industry and social networks have between them also created a highly intrusive and opaque environment for consumers. Individual web-surfers are tracked, their interests analysed, their consumption habits and desires addressed by behavioural targeting through a range of advertising networks and solutions. Few of these delight us yet and many of them still annoy. Despite the flamboyant smoke and mirrors of the advertising industry, it is still a common experience to be bombarded for weeks online by advertisements for products we have already purchased. Big data simply allows some of these existing databases to be overlaid upon one another in ways which will undoubtedly reveal even more insights into consumer behaviours and tastes.

If we were to re-imagine the development of systems across networks that aligned the business models of the network operators and those that sold services across them, we should be able to both reduce friction in process, improve consumer experiences and increase commercial margins. If it were that simple, however, we might just have seen it happen already. There are, of course, problems. Identifying the nature of every transaction taking place across a network represents a significant invasion of privacy. What seems worse is that creating the kind of control over the network that would facilitate that level of monitoring would lead to a rapid erosion of Net Neutrality. Those who understand the architectural changes that have occurred to the internet in recent years, through the development of Content Distribution Networks (CDNs) and through the imposition of iNAT controls on network gateways, suggest that Net Neutrality is already massively eroded if not already almost mythical. Yet, the concept of Net Neutrality remains key to the open environment that has spawned so much innovation and online entrepreneurship. Commercial developments that threaten a core of net neutrality will in the end, be self-defeating.

An open web was the key to making this level playing field accessible and essential to that was the creation of a set of protocols that could allow large numbers of relatively technically unskilled folk to build meaningful online presence. The trend towards digital medievalism increasingly threatens the open web. The massive popularity of app development for closed platforms like IoS or even for less closed ones like Android, moves focus away from the web's naturally collaborative environment into something more siloed. Arguably lower level open API availability represents the growing solution to enabling collaborative opportunities while still only offering functionally dedicated applications. So there is a delicate balance to strike between retaining openness and low barriers to entry and enabling an internet-wide capability to detect, monitor, track and monetise all predefined network transactions.

The model would also of course require content creators and service managers to share revenue with the operators and bandwidth providers. It would be naive to underestimate the complexity of commercial negotiations required to achieve this. Yet, despite all these challenges, I believe that ultimately this will be the way forward for content in the digital economy. The reason for my certainty is because of the powerful commercial imperative to reduce friction in digital markets. Digital marketplaces thrive on the free flow of data across them, the more impedance introduced, the higher the price to manage and transact.

Music has become particularly complex in its rights landscape. The collaborative nature of song-writing and music creation is now commonplace. Co-creation is the nature of the game. Bands collectively write the music, pen the words, create the videos, design the costume, stage-set, and brand extension all the way through to new life-style fads like designing a band-branded beer. But of course individual contributors do more or less. Some only write the words, some only write the music, some only perform, some only drink the beer. The industry tradition of separating all these credits into separate rights, negotiating complex and opaque contractual arrangements for them separately, managing those rights separately and creating an industry wide infrastructure all around the world to administer separate rights separately, looks increasingly archaic. That kind of inefficiency is crying out to be reformed. The business of co-creation would be much better served by holistic, comprehensive rights databases, not separate ones that enforce divisions and charge rates on different bases with statutory instruments brought to bear on some sets of rights and prices but not on others. The legacy offers a broken model. Trying to fix that legacy will never work. A new architecture needs to be built not just for music but for the other digital media sectors too.

By way of comparison, the world of the printed book, for a long time during the early impact of the internet, looked upon music as a poor and less well-educated relation. Today, book publishers find themselves in a position not dissimilar to the music industry. The massive investment that Amazon has made in the Kindle platform has driven digital sales of books singlehandedly. All the other efforts to compete, like Apple's ebooks, the Kobo open reader, or the Sony ebook platform have failed to make the same level of impact. Even in 2007, there were six or seven competing ebook platforms, but Amazon saw the opportunity early enough, bought Mobipocket, a startup e-reader software company, and their software formed the basis of the Kindle. It was not without cost, but several hundred million dollars of investment led Amazon to its current dominance. Publishers like music companies are now contemplating massive price erosion and a collapsing high street retail channel. Amazon recently featured the top 100 bestselling new novelson sale for a limited promotion at 20pence each. The share of digital titles sold to print titles is growing rapidly and although it some way off the 50% that is the case for music in the US at the time of writing, the trend is unmistakeable.

Amazon's dominance may have been prevented if more than one platform had been encouraged, but the book publishers failed to acknowledge the importance early enough to prevent the company dominating the market. At the time, perhaps they were too busy trying to prevent Google from the mass digitization of their catalogues. Publishers began to realise in late 2009 early 2010 that the effect of the Kindle was to create a walled garden - one of the many that Amazon is creating to form its digital city state. At first, the trade publishing divisions of the big publishing houses tried to sabotage the efforts of their own internal digital publishing divisions. They tried to make them sell digital titles at a higher price than print. Then, when that clearly failed, they thought they might take a leaf out of music's book and turn to another digital city state for protection. In 2010, Apple agreed a deal to sell the major publisher's digital books on an agency model. This was based on a simple concept that instead of the retailer fixing the price paid by the consumer, the publisher would do so and the retailer, in this case the iTunes Store, would simply charge their 30% commission on top. The publishers felt that this was a viable means of maintaining price points. Unfortunately, for a variety of reasons which became embarrassing for the book trade, this initiative led to a US Department of Justice investigation. The book industry was seen to be acting against the anti-trust regulations, attempting to fix the market. Ironically of course this ruling was to the direct benefit of Amazon whose sales continued to grow in double digits.

The pain in much of this may for the moment seem greater for the publishers than for the authors, many of whom unlike musicians whose contracts make no concessions to digital, seem to have created contracts that yield as much money from ebooks as from paperbooks. Furthermore, hardback buyers still represent a valuable piece of market share. Some say they represent a demographic who will not die off for another generation - so the massive shifts in format preferences have left some authors at least, in roughly the same place economically as they were before. The publishers themselves however are faced with growing cost-structures and reducing margins which seem to demand industry consolidation to achieve scale and major company restructuring which will start to undermine the primacy of the publishing house itself. We have recently seen the acquisition of Penguin books by Random House in what was explicitly a move to gain more scale and therefore more market leverage against Amazon. Similarly in the world of advertising, the media buying world has been shaken by the merger of the Omincom Group and the Publicis Group. The consolidation was again explained as a means of creating greater market leverage to compete more effectively with the new advertising giants of Google and Facebook. Welcome to what I call the digital medieval world.

7. Digital Medieval

The digital medieval world is dominated by four giants, Google, Amazon, Facebook, Apple (GAFA). Twitter may soon join it as it powers through its initial public offering. They are reshaping not just the digital media economy, but the entire face of advertising and consumer relations. The GAFA companies want consumers to be as plugged into them as they can be. Consumers are beginning to react against this by trying to get as unplugged as possible, but that is still a small if growing trend. The digital medieval landscape is made up of digital city-states grown up out of the walled gardens of today and the massive up-swing in individual, boutique offerings that may or may not align themselves with any of the big states. Consumers are either locked into their own preferred digital city-states enjoying the ease of use, frictionless commerce and simplicity that provides, or they roam from digital city-state to digital city-state, tethered to none and increasingly feeling the inconvenience of the lack of interoperability encouraged between them.

As new digital services develop and competition between them increases, the desire for different forms of consumer lock-in increases. As Apple launches its long awaited streaming music service to compete with Spotify and Deezer, it is also intended to decrease the need for residents of Apple's walled garden to leave its sunlit slopes. This is a typical driver that makes the walls of the gardens rise. Digital medieval is where you get to when the walls of the walled-gardens become so high you can't climb over them anymore, but it is also a cultural experience arising from the dizzying onward rush of innovation and an accompanying natural reaction against that.

In the medieval period, as a result of the collapse of the Holy Roman Empire, much of the sophistication of previous centuries was lost. Villages, communities, entire nations lost collective memory of the rules, wisdom and morality that had preceded them. In the digital medieval period we have proliferated more data than in the entire previous history of the planet. We currently are starting to derive small amounts of knowledge from analyzing that data. We painfully piece together half-complete narratives that help us navigate our continually changing digital world. From these thin layers of new knowledge, even scarcer amounts of wisdom are derived. The speed of innovation has given the world a degree of collective amnesia. The vertiginous rise of progress is accompanied by a sinking apprehension at our loss of understanding. The wisdom that came from continuity and experience gets eroded in the digital medieval period. The global village elders, to whom we may have looked in the past for guidance, struggle to find voices in this new environment.

For consumers, the digital medieval period may not be a dark age entirely without education, but it is an anarchic and fractious world in which, if balance and humanity are to survive, the organic authenticity of small companies will collectively face many challenges from the walled cities of the major brands. Most mainstream consumers will struggle to leave the walled cities they enter, seduced into staying in by loss-leader goods and low-ball pricing. More affluent consumers will find themselves increasingly drawn to graze among the carefully manicured and curated offerings of niche producers out in the fields.

Interestingly in this scenario, state support and encouragement of the small and medium sized enterprises outside the digital city-states will face new challenges. The current fashion for incentivizing rapid high growth businesses with hockey stick revenue models is firmly rooted in the successes of the dot com boom and its accompanying greed. Whether it be venture capital or government programs, the favorite target is the early stage starry start-up who can zoom meteor-like into economic visibility and contribution. Encouraging companies who employ ten people to grow fast on the global internet stage and start employing one hundred workers is the standard approach of the day. The classic exit route for these meteoric companies is to be acquired quickly by the GAFA city-states of digital medievalism. Alongside the boom and buy cycle lurks the cottage industry of one or two person companies who may number hundreds, thousands or even millions across the planet as a whole. They may be individual service providers, consultants, craftspeople, working musicians or bands or new digital makers of different kinds. As a whole sector their contribution is significant too, but their need for support is very different. They have slow-burn, long-stay economic cycles where margins are low but so are overheads, where life-style, collaboration, co-creation and openness may have as much to do with success as rapid scaling. Sector companies in this kind of environment benefit from shared access to facilities, open standards and interoperability of systems to enable greater and more variable collaboration.

Market pressure to grow and expand will force the GAFA city-states of the web and their successors, to seek even greater dominance in our lives. They will integrate more vertically, seeking to take greater ownership of services, which form essential parts of the fabric of daily life. Once they outgrow their own media markets and begin to penetrate other economic sectors, then these towering digital city-states will also be compelled to integrate with large infrastructure players like AT&T, Comcast or Liberty. Then, indeed, they will seek to move into large-scale transport, logistics or medical care businesses. The Google Fiber experiments with hyper high-speed broadband in Kansas and its driverless car experiments on the roads of California already indicate the direction. The only thing that is less clear is the degree of integration and interoperation. It's not that consumers won't have choice and that open platforms won't offer similar or competing offers, but the closed, gleaming cities of Apple or Amazon will offer convenience, ease of use and low prices for an increasingly broad range of goods and services. They will dominate our lives. Consumers in the "mainstream" will be forced into even deeper forms of brand loyalty, which even as they reflect their demographic profiles may also start to define their individual identities. The tribes of Android or Apple consumers already feel themselves led to different places on the digital plains.

    As they compete, the giants of GAFA will start to drive further away from interoperability and more towards proprietary, exclusive solutions. It is already becoming difficult to get Google and Apple applications, even at a core level like calendars and contacts to talk to one another. Consumers were the victims of the Apple "maps debacle" as the company tried to reduce its dependency on Google. These fundamental disjunctures about the very basics of perception, what time of day it is, when we should meet and where geographically we are located, are reminders of earlier eras when the fundamentals of world-views clashed violently and different regimes tried to impose different calendars on the world. In the digital medieval world these matters are managed or mis-managed, with more sophistication, more akin to Orwell's 1984 than the Spanish Inquisition, but the nature and vulnerability of a teenager's life today whose social interactions are insidiously ruled by Facebook and Twitter is hard to ignore.

Music, entertainment and basic utilities have been the cornerstones, the loss-leaders which led down the primrose path to the walled gardens. In the coming years, what used to be walled gardens will become the city states and will expand to cater for broader aspects of our lives from entertainment to education, to dining out, to travel, to energy management, personal and domestic security, health and well-being. Some developments will involve a healthy introduction of transparency. Pricing of products in these kinds of subscription environments may well become more driven by the full length of the value chain. So for example, we might start to see streaming media services priced according to their actual energy consumption levels as well as just their bandwidth use. Cloud computing services, like digital lockers, have to take into account the cost of energy consumption in doing things like keeping the servers cool, in charging for the service. Where latency is less of an issue and you can afford to use a service driven out of a server in the Arctic, it will be less expensive than one where more locally situated servers incur higher electricity costs to keep the servers cool. Maybe you would simply like to act as an individualized market research bot and report all your consumption habits back to Amazon or Facebook in exchange for free functionality or special discounts? Similarly you can get a discount on your car insurance if you allow a black box to be mounted to track your every movement, acceleration and screaming halt. As this digital transference occurs across different elements of our economic and social lives, so consumers will find themselves encouraged to stay locked inside the walls of one or other of the digital city states whether they belong to Amazon, Apple or Google or new entrants whose identities we are yet to discover. Older players like Microsoft, or Sony will struggle to regain lost ground or increase their share.

Newer entrants like Samsung, Facebook, Twitter and their descendants may burst onto the scene with increasing speed.

While, the glistening towers of the digital city-states will providing compelling environments and solutions for the many, they will not simply host the cultural products of the major studios and labels. They will also be interested in more niche offerings and talent that emerges from individual cultural efforts. Conversely, there will be also the tastemakers, the young and the very poor, the rich and the rebels, who will reject any of the homogeneity of city-states on principle. Perhaps too, we will see refugees fleeing from large-scale disasters that, from time to time will be bound to occur in the city-states, like irregularities in personal data security or billing issues, or even more fundamental things such as the food-supply or sanitation systems. They will be drawn to browse the myriad niche, small-holdings that populate the rest of the web. Increasingly paranoid concerns about privacy and trust will also lead to an erosion of public confidence in the value of participating in city-states services. On the digital medieval plains, the sight of entire denizens of one city state that has failed, being migrated to a new incumbent may become more frequent too - Bebo anybody?

The implications of digital medieval also extend to legislation and democracy. We live in a world of considerable and increasing complexity, most of which is driven by the rapid rate of technological change. The effect of this on legislation is significant in a digital medieval context because the law finds it very hard to keep up. The legislative requirement to make laws that are sufficiently broadly applicable as to be generic starts to break down in this kind of environment. The fact is that drafting laws for all of copyright and patent applications has become increasingly challenging. In recent UK legislation on the digital economy, specific carve outs of the law were made, for example, for photographers. Lawmakers at once recognized that their generic lawmaking was still required and yet this one subcategory needed to be excluded. As discussed above, copyright reform has progressed by the multiplication of series of exceptions, not by addressing the fundamental issues.

The process of drafting, amendment and debate, in this digital and complex context becomes increasingly questionable as a democratic process. First, the sophistication and complexity of real world activities makes it less and less common for those debating new legislation to understand the detail or real affect of what changes they are contemplating. Unintended consequences of new laws become increasingly frequent. In the currently over-populated House of Lords, there are too many peers who are not qualified by real commercial experience or public service, but are there because they have been politically favored, and vote accordingly. The combination of favor peerages and the traditional inherited peers seems to outweigh the worthy minority who has valid real world experience and professional qualifications. This means that the vested interests of lobbyists receive a disproportionate amount of influence since they are the ones who can take the time to educate a politician into the detail of a particular case. The particular hazard in copyright law of a mode of reform driven by the introduction of layer upon layer of exceptions, means that the law itself simply becomes more complex. This is in the interests of no one, neither rights holders, nor creators nor consumers. Those that do benefit of course are the legal fraternity themselves. In the digital medieval world, it has become increasingly difficult for politicians to retain a moral compass. Their inability to navigate the choppy waters of immensely fast change, leads to a kind of enforced ignorance that ends up making bad or unimplementable laws - an early example of this might be the UK's Digital Economy Act.

The generic nature of lawmaking in the UK is inevitably made necessary by limited parliamentary time. It has always been justified on the basis that judgments and precedents could be established by case law, which would refine it and allow for the flexing needed to deal with unfolding complexity and specificity of context. Unfortunately, as we know in the vertiginous digital medieval world, the rate of change is so rapid that precedent itself may become increasingly difficult to apply. How can you find precedent for a world so fundamentally changed that it is literally unprecedented?

This growing lack of moral compass and lack of useful precedent are characteristics of a medieval environment. It threatens the stability of democracy because ordinary people increasingly come across the inadequacy of lawmaking in the face of their own experiences in their ordinary lives. This growing gap between the perceptions of people on the street and those that would seek to create meaningful governance is a recipe for social unrest. In the last few years, the growth of civil unrest has become a global phenomenon. The Occupy demonstrations, the riots of the summer of 2011 in the UK, the Arab spring, social unrest in Spain and Greece, in Brazil and in the US were each provoked by different specific local conditions and circumstances. These were a variety of revolts against a variety of causes. Triggered by a desire to protest the credit crunch or a no-longer-bearable dictatorship, all of these struggles were organized and amplified by social media platforms such as Twitter and Facebook. Taken as a whole, they suggest an alarming picture of the inability of existing systems of governance and political regimes to contain the growing turmoil of the populace provoked by rapid socio-economic change which is itself driven by new technological capabilities that seem increasingly at odds with what the law has to offer. This is not suggesting that social-media platforms are essentially subversive, but that they enable public sentiment to be organized, disseminated and amplified in real-time and in dynamic response to changing circumstances in ways which have not been previously seen by either governments or citizens. The technological capability is there to aid the disruption of whole societies as well commerce.

Digital medieval may ultimately simply be a useful metaphor, a historical and linguistic lens through which to better understand our current condition. It does display however some remarkably useful correlation to contemporary circumstances. My friend and colleague, Professor Evelyn Welch of Kings College, London has often argued that we should be able to draw on historical insights and analysis of earlier periods of history to explain and illuminate the present day. I have frequently argued that this is absurd and that the massive degree of progress and societal change in values, education, health, technology and above all human ambition renders such analogies irrelevant. As I have pursued this digital medieval argument in talks and discussions, I have come to the conclusion that Professor Welch might be right. Perhaps we do need the urgent help of scholars of the medieval and renaissance periods to help us understand how to move forward on a global basis to avoid entering a darker era and instead help reach a level of greater enlightenment.

Digital Medieval Music

Back in the world of music, those few, carefully selected bands signed to the few remaining major labels will also find themselves compelled to address their fans through digital city-state driven brand alliances. Credibility used to make bands shy away from working with brands; economic stringency has reduced that resistance considerably. Digital city state businesses will commit them to it.

Out in the fields, there will be a continued proliferation of direct to fan platforms like Musicglue and Bandcamp and other enabling technologies. They will allow thousands of bands and individual artists, like medieval troubadours wondering the digital and the actual countryside, to create their own fan-bases and grow their own communities through live performance, video airplay and social media. In this, there is clearly a degree of interdependence and crossover too. Crowd funding continues to lower the barriers to entry into the market and the cost of music production equipment continues to decrease, so increasingly bands will be appearing in little venues or festivals near you. Equally, the draw and kudos of the major labels will continue to act as both a benchmark of achievement and a financial magnet.

These few remaining global labels are already part of larger corporate groupings - Universal within Vivendi - Sony Music within Sony Corporation. So far Warner Music under its new private ownership stands as a lone independent and we will see whether that gives it particular strengths or abilities. The trend though is likely to be that these entertainment units become more absorbed into the infrastructure and economy of the digital cities. There they will create a few highly valued, massively promoted global music stars.

Over the last twenty years, the IFPI has reported a visible shift towards local repertoire and away from global acts. Existing global mega-artists are selling fewer albums. That is a trend, which will continue. Increasingly the global pop acts will come from very commercial "talent events" like Pop Idol and the X Factor. The contrived nature of those kinds of artists is going to move popular taste further and further away from the style of community driven musicians grown out in the fields. Major labels will act as digital city-states too. This will become more apparent from an artists perspective as they increasingly demand participation in all aspects of an artist's career. Vivendi recently acquired an online ticketing platform called SeeTickets. In the wake of this, it seems likely that all artists signed to Universal labels will be expected as a matter of course to sell their online tickets for their shows through SeeTickets.

It is not yet clear what this bifurcation of music, between the highly commercial and the virtually de-industrialized will do for the quality of music. Quality in culture is something, which few of us agree on, but most of us recognize when we hear it. A unique combination of originality and musical ability, capturing audio pathways of the brain, creating the new reverberations of the cultural, social moment and twisting them in new directions. Quality originality and talent may remain as elusive as ever, but to a degree, I am optimistic that sheer numbers and energy combined with the wider accessibility of audiences is enriching the diversity of the musical scene.

When there are so many new sounds, you certainly need help in deciding what to listen to. In this anarchic landscape, the importance of music discovery is set to grow. There are plenty of companies trying to solve the problem of discovering new bands and new talent. There are all kinds of solutions on offer, driven either by human curation or by algorithmic analysis of fan behaviours - most often a combination of both. A subtle but significant difference is growing between discovery (helping you find stuff yourself) and recommendations (suggesting things you will like). Success remains elusive. It will come from those whose recommendations are not only better than 80% right, but also less than 20% alienatingly wrong.

As the music industry rebuilds itself as a cottage industry of small companies speckling the digital landscape, then the companies themselves may have a greater role to play as curators. Instead of being invisible and behind the scenes, some will find success by embracing a fuller direct relationship with fans.

Music companies may begin to recover value from some of those basic functions of a "label" - to inform fans of the provenance and make-up of the music. Just as I want to know what farm my beef came from or what field these plums were grown in. Some labels were always brands such as Blue Note, Motown or 4AD - even Stiff! They came to define a genre of music and launched careers with the endorsement they lent to new artists. Like contemporary art, understanding the context from which music comes, increases its value. As the variety and quantity of music proliferates across the web, the value of a label as brand will increase. With such a massive diversity of content to choose from, even sophisticated niche consumers need reliable curators as endorsers of style, genre and quality.

But it may not be a matter of labels doing the curation and the aggregation. One of the great attractions of crowd-sourced funding is that it facilitates the fan base. It is not just that a band raises a few hundred thousand dollars, they also build a loyal community of support that stays with them and wants in on the next project. The strength of Pledgemusic is that it can provide that great platform for the artist. The problem is that it is insufficiently discriminating for the fans. So in the digital medieval future, maybe this kind of function will be more finely positioned from a consumer perspective, by genre, by gender, by geography.

Music has been set free on the web, but like all freed slaves it begins life with almost nothing. It will continue to be enriched by waves of innovation and as this happens,   its commercial and cultural value will gradually return. Music can travel further round the globe than ever. It can evolve and interact between fans in new and startlingly beautiful ways. It can go viral in days. Social media may spread the word about music, it may also be used to manipulate how it sounds. Brian Eno, has been working on a product which creates music that shifts and changes in accordance with listener feedback on social networks. Others are experimenting with sensory or bio-feedback that changes the music as your body reacts to it. As computing power grows and big data becomes more manageable and manipulable in real time, the opportunities are growing to explore these kinds of feedback-loops in real time via individual behaviour or collectively as part of a live event.

Digital medievalism will be nothing if not vivid. The quality of image and audio which we experience will continue to intensify. Whereas the first effects of mp3 audio compression were to increase mobility at the cost of quality, fans are increasingly looking for better audio. The shift from commuters wearing tiny earbuds to the current fashion for larger headphones is not just a retro, throwback to the '80s, it is an indicator that consumers want greater immersion, greater escapism and better quality audio to make the experience more authentic. Digital medievalism will increase our range and our memory of music even if it may also confuse us as to the exact provenance of what we stumble upon.

As Oliver Sachs has set out so poignantly in Musicophilia, music moves us in primitive ways. It reaches us through parts of our brain laid down on a separate track from our language, maths, science, visual understandings. Whatever happens to the music industry in the next twenty years, our emotional responses to music will remain among the most powerful we ever experience. No amount of online innovation will change that. As long as we continue to invent new ways of making, discovering and relating to music, we will learn more about the superpowers music possesses, collectively and individually, to connect us to our pasts and help shape our futures.

Digital medievalism represents an increasingly likely scenario of how our experiences online will develop. In the face of this less than appetising future, nation states need to consider seriously how best to navigate the new landscape. The digital city states now effectively perform fundamental, infrastructural roles in sustaining global online commerce and culture. To what kinds of governance or regulation they should be subjected is far from clear despite the growing appetite for it. The opportunity to turn the digital medieval period into the digital renaissance is great, it would be unfortunate if we had to wait centuries for it to emerge.

8. Digital renaissance

Music's transition to the internet and an entirely digital business model is almost complete. It may never become entirely digital. CD sales continue to represent as much as 50% of the business even today in parts of the world. Although the trend is clearly away from physical product towards digital, the physical may never entirely disappear. Vinyl sales have been on the increase in recent years which is probably an indicator of the kind of Maker-community led, return to a desire for the self-made, the more personalised, more authentic product. A music producer friend of mine recently bought a vinyl lathe cutter to create his own platters. The renaissance may not be entirely digital.

The games business has been one hundred percent digital from the outset, but it has its own shift to endure, from console to online. Newspapers and magazines have seen their revenues decimated by the shift of advertising from their pages to the internet. Conversely, the television industry has been buoyed up by increased viewing figures in the major markets and by an advertising industry which is keen to support traditional models, promote the liveness of sport and other forms of "event television" in the face of reduced margins and Google's online dominance. The film industry has seen its revenues from DVDs plummet, because of file-sharing it would argue, and has yet to find a way of translating its services online. Ebooks and in particular Amazon's aggressive Kindle strategy, have begun to allow book publishers to feel their way into an online world with, for now, slightly less pain than music endured. There is still some way to go in the transition of these businesses. While the music industry may be starting to see the early glimmers of an age of enlightenment, light at the end of the tunnel, the rest of the digital media world is still in its medieval period.

Ironically, having lived through the dark ages when it seemed creative work had no value, competition for content and an authentic connection to the creator, may just turn out to be the triggers of enlightenment. As the creative industries emerge from their dark ages, they will find the new ways to create new demand for their stories, movies, music, and games. The long tail of small businesses creating unique content will grow in the face of consolidating major studios and publishing houses. Interestingly, there are also signs that technological shifts may also play into this. The consumer electronics companies and the telecos wishing to resist the power of the digital city-states may try to proliferate uptake of their own operating systems - they are already starting to do this. Samsung has officially announced its Tizen OS and Palm's Web OS, once acquired by HP and then dropped, has been bought by LG, a Korean consumer electronics manufacturer, to be used as the operating system in connected TVs. If this trend of multiplying operating system continues, the first effect will be to make content creation for devices more expensive to produce again. Developers will be back to having to make multiple installs and tweaks for operation on different platforms just as they had to in the early days of smart mobile phone handset proliferation. Secondarily, however, it may herald a new faith in open web standards like HTML5 to foster interoperability in the digital renaissance.

Even as the prospect grows of the web vanishing completely in a digital medieval meltdown of apps and walled gardens, the competitors to the digital city states may just begin to shift the balance. A similar tension between the familiar poles of open and proprietary solutions has often been a catalyst in software and technological innovation. If we are to progress from digital medievalism to digital renaissance, then open platforms and open standards may well turn out to be key. They will be the means by which new creative work can be produced and delivered to all devices and all environments without being rendered unprofitable by the kind of 30% claw-back revenue shares demanded inside the digital city states. At the very least, we will continue to see these different solutions co-existing and competing.

A truly open digital renaissance will have to be an interoperable renaissance. City states and small free-holders will organise around single cross-platform solutions. It will be a flowering of innovation and creativity, inspired by the richness of experiences that the internet and digital platforms can offer. Tablets, phablets, phones and TVs become a tapestry of screens across which media will be pervasive. The digital renaissance will witness a fluidity and an ease of access to content of all kinds whether its news and weather information, a game we obsess on, a movie we take with us on the road or our vacation image stream. Seamless transmission of personalised experiences will become the norm, from static home device to mobile in-transit device to office screen, to the screens in the homes of friends and families.

The ability to move our content around with us, seamlessly in real time from device to device, from screen to screen will also increase our collective consumption levels both in what we watch together and in what we pass along or recommend. The concepts of super-distribution where each consumer also becomes a retailer may well return in the digital renaissance. It may not take the literal and mechanistic form that the founders of Intertrust tried to instil in their efforts, first time around at the Secure Digital Music Initiative, but in the name of their company is a clue to how it may occur. Trust, sharing, value and payment will become the finest and most sophisticated layers of the new creative economy. In the digital medieval period, the concept of forcing someone to pay remains very strongly in place inside the digital city states. Out in the fields among the maker community, the couch surfers, the air b'n'b travellers and the troubadour musicians like Amanda Palmer who crowd-fund their work, a new culture of barter and reputation develops which will become more sophisticated in the digital renaissance.

One of the big unanswered questions today is whether the nature of trust, barter and reputation-based systems can scale. Can a sharing economy come to scale without being spoofed and faked out of existence? Will the powers of the digital city states themselves encourage and protect the growth of the sharing economy? If they are mindful of its power they will encourage it on their own platforms - and that might be prove compromising too. With careful governance and the right balance of freedom and moderation, we can create value exchanges that are not based on pure economic metrics but, working at scale across broader segments of the economy, could function sufficiently powerfully to change radically the basis of economic growth. That non-fiscal approach might just turn out to be one of the defining characteristics of a digital renaissance.

Online culture and legacy

More than ten years before the web began, in 1985, my first contact with the music industry was as a researcher at the National Sound Archive. Our task was to collect a copy of every commercial recording released in the UK, but without the benefit enjoyed by librarians of what is called Statutory Deposit - the legal requirement on publishers to deposit a copy of each new book with the British Library. As a result of this, Archive staff had to make periodical visits to major record companies to persuade them to put the Archive on their distribution list for promotional copies of new releases. I joined one of the archivists on a visit to meet the late Maurice Oberstein, the Chairman of Polygram Records. He was a colourful New Yorker, well known in the industry for his dog Eric who accompanied him everywhere and for the strange vocal tic that turned his voice into a falsetto whenever he became exercised by something.

We entered his long narrow office, its walls lined with shelves of CDs. "Obie" sat at his desk, at the far end of the room and, as if in some strange reference to the famous dog and gramophone logo of His Masters Voice, he addressed all his comments to his dog. We explained our mission to him, that we were from the Sound Archive collecting recordings for posterity, that subsequent generations would be grateful for his actions, that his CDs represented an unparalleled cultural record, that would be invaluable to future researchers. He tilted his head to one side, enquiringly of his dog who lazily lifted an ear. We continued to explain that we would be very appreciative if he could start having all his new releases sent to the Archive for us to preserve for future generations. He looked over at us and back at Eric. One of them growled. Then he turned and said, in a bark that turned mid-sentence into a falsetto yelp: "You have five minutes to take as many CDs off these shelves as you can - and then get the hell out of my office!" We left without taking a single CD, our tails between our legs, but several weeks later the flow of releases from Polygram resumed and the Archive's collections continued without interruption.

Obie recognised that making donations to posterity was an obligation to culture he could not afford to ignore. He realised that while making money from music was a commercial reality for all involved in the industrial process, the cultural contribution made by the music his industry produced was also a source of its enduring value. In the 21st Century as we digitise our books, photographs, music, and movies, forward thinkers have started to worry that these totems of cultural identity might disappear altogether. We are all gradually throwing out our old paperbacks, DVDs and CDs. We reason that they are all available from the Amazon cloud, or on Spotify, on iTunes, on the Kindle. The digital city states have also become the global custodians of the planet's cultural history. The Google Books project has an ambition more vast than the great Library of Alexandria. Of course, some will still individually collect beautifully bound or illustrated books, amazingly packaged rare albums or unique artworks. Every middle-class home is a mini-museum of personally curated taste, but this idea may fade and in the next generation it may vanish altogether. Humans are collectors and exhibitionists. When we all complete our transitions to a digital world, we may feel a massive sense of loss at not having these symbols of cultural identity and achievement online. That is the motivation for the Google Books project, but questions of access and openness arise rapidly in this context. Who will get a library pass to the digital Alexandria and at what price?

The internet revolution still has a long way to go before it can develop the means to enable a richness of presence to provide average consumers (not specialist bloggers, writers, tweeters or other online mavens) with a full means of signalling my cultural identity to others. Profile pages and avatars, pin-drops, image streams, and public playlists proliferate but so far my online status remains a thin substitute for the visceral patina of physical objects on a bookshelf in the living room. A Facebook Like is a pale indicator of cultural taste or it may simply demonstrate that you are victim to another spoof. It may be there as a token of my passion or simply by accident, tricked into existence by some mischievous marketing app. To misquote Paul Simon, it's still nascent after all of these years.

The challenge of online identity extends to digital media even after death. When folk die today, their descendants currently experience troubling online challenges. Digital documents, music, images and video may all reside somewhere in the cloud. The passwords of the deceased may go with them to the grave, rendering digital legacies unobtainable. Archivists already wring their hands that word-processed literature, digitally edited film or music scores, leave precious little behind in the form of the hand amended manuscripts or early takes of recordings, betraying the iterations of the creative process that scholars love to study. The same applies when someone may wish to memorialise a deceased parent or simply inherit their online music collection. Digital culture requires digital legacy.

Major online service operators have, from time to time, been prompted to explore these matters. In September 2012, considerable discussion was generated when, the Sunday Times, a UK newspaper, reported that Bruce Willis was about to sue iTunes whose license would prevent him (and the rest of us) from passing on his "purchased" music collection to his children. The story turned out to be a fake, which made its own point, but it enlivened the debate and raised the issue. The topic can hardly have been high on business agendas at the outset, but it is an important element in the development of digital culture now. Digital heaven or digital archive, these issues around continued access and ownership have not been resolved. Sites like ifidie.net and 1000memories.com offer some kind of web memorial. They offer the consumer the chance to create their own digital archives of their lives, designed to survive them. Others have experimented with enabling creation of a hologram of a loved one, based on their personal data to be produced after their death like a kind of digital cryogenic reconstruction. This would certainly be interesting, but it would not redeem the particular curation of music, books and art by which we identify ourselves. It would be a sad destiny if, after our deaths, large parts of our digital assets simply sat in limbo until the subscription ran out and then returned silently and anonymously to the services who supplied them. Equally, as company integrate vertically inside digital city states perhaps that is a way that death will be managed. Spotify funeral services anyone? The idea certainly gives "my funeral playlist" a whole new potential - no subscription complete without one.

In the digital renaissance, online culture will continue to develop its own powerful social dimension. If a musician can perform a duet with the recorded voice of her own father, then we should all be able to access and engage with our own digital pasts. I suspect, however, that the public correlation of online and offline reputation may be a more commercial catalyst to achieving a form of online preservation. The first striking occurrence of this was when, in the summer of 2012, deceased artist, Tupac Shakur, "appeared" on-stage with live performers Snoop Dogg and Dr Dre at Coachella, an outdoor music festival. The video went viral across the web and, at the time of writing, has been viewed by over 14 million people. Gizmodo, a web geek blog, reported gleefully that this was not actually a hologram, but a computer graphics effect combined with a 19th century glass and light trick, literally smoke and mirrors. As the Gizmodo journalist observed: "With all the weed and ecstasy throbbing through Coachella, there were probably a good number of fans who thought they were actually witnessing a reincarnation". Studios have long toyed with the idea of duets between dead artists and their successors, one of the most dramatic came as early as 1991, when Natalie Cole sang "with" her late father Nat King Cole. The choice of song was "Unforgettable". The appetite is undoubtedly there for online preservation, but so far it remains mainly in the domain of stars. For the mass of others, the web will make it less likely than in the past, that a scholar will make an accidental discovery of a trove of documents revealing some great insight into a previously unknown musician. The ease of copying on the internet is accompanied by an equal and opposite ease of erasure.

A different kind of benefit in the form of new digital formats, rich media environments and multi-dimensional media products will begin to flower in the digital renaissance. Collaborative communities will redefine co-creation. Social media may spread the word about music, it may also be used to manipulate how it sounds. The relationship between video, games, and music will continue to deepen. Vyclone, a mobile video company, allows fans at a gig, each to film their own clips of a show on their phones which are then assembled on the fly and edited for sharing in real time. Industrial Light and Magic, a special effects company, are now able to use the same digital assets with the same high resolution in an interactive game as in a movie as in a TV show. Facial recognition in games, compared with increasingly ultra-realistic rendering and advanced motion capture capabilities are all driving towards more immersive and compelling game environments. Each of these elements will be driven by online interactivity in different ways, allowing consumers to be able to project themselves digitally inside the very game environments that they are playing. Virtual reality had a brief flowering in the 90s only to subside again. The digital renaissance will certainly see a resurgence in the vivid creation of digital game and entertainment environments in which illusion and reality will become more closely fused.

As the world geo-economic balance shifts, more experiments involving film, games and music from different countries will reflect the change. The eyes of the west will turn increasingly east. Cultural mash ups in different styles and formats will increasingly provoke and entertain. Psy, the Korean pop phenomenon whose Gangnam Style track did not exactly announce the beginning of a wave of Asian influence will nonetheless be seen as an early example of a new kind of mashed-up global cultural renaissance. Political awareness of the power of music and culture to move masses will inevitably also accompany this shift. Digital medievalism brings with it a new degree of politicisation of culture. Between the worlds of crowd-created Baauer Harlem Shake videos and Disney controlled-circulation cartoons appears to be a widening gap. Certain political regimes will once again run scared of music's power and seek to suppress it. The Russian female punk band, Pussy Power, who were arrested for performing a song in a Moscow cathedral, critical of the president, received two year prison sentences despite global protests in their defence. Inevitably, we will see more of this kind of cultural limitation in regimes where open expression is still not the norm.

The web, the internet, the mp3 (and its video counterparts) have thrown into flux so many traditional relationships; hardware and software devices, high street and virtual retail, physical and digital content, local and global services, fixed and mobile platforms, publishers and retailers, producers and consumers of creative work. What started out as subversive and underground has become mass market. Transformation occurs at different speeds and in shifting patterns across different parts of our economy and culture. We have unleashed upon ourselves a new era of opportunity for simultaneous enrichment and impoverishment. Some of us started out as cyber punks, then became entrepreneurs and may end up needing to become philosophers of the digital age. As we contemplate the future, however, our choices are increasingly stark between a growing darkness of global cyber strife and data lock-ins or an enticing , open digital enlightenment. The split is between increased privatisation of our identities, digital city state competitiveness and embattlement or a more trusting, reputation-based community centred on openess and transferability.

The delta is widening, between a move further down into digital medievalism or an ascent to a digital renaissance. Now more than ever we need to take a strategic and philosophical view of the world. The large digital city-state companies such as Google and Facebook may not contain inherently evil people. I am quite convinced that all of them as individuals wish to do good things, but their scale works against them. The company as organism takes on its own direction, unleashes its own unintended consequences. The status of the internet giants has become deeply ambiguous. As titans of the global economy they have undue influence over what happens, but no one nation state is able to coordinate with enough others to regulate them. Global internet companies have more reach even than the US or the EU. The onus on them to act responsibly may begin to rest heavily on their shareholder obligations. Regulators, executives and consumers, in the face of all this, must continue affirmatively to improve and to improvise, to take risks and to take seriously the duty of care, to be courageous and compassionate, to trust one another and above all to continue to make it up as we go along. Digital medieval or digital renaissance? Can collective action and community response to changes in social media platforms succeed in modelling their owners into the model of that more open democracy would wish to see or the one their shareholder-value imperative drives them towards? The choice is not just in the hands of companies and governments. Ultimately the choice is in our hands as consumers and voters.

Coda: The Mariachi of Mexico City

The cantina is so loud; you can barely hear the music coming from one band as it merges into the sounds of the other. There are three in-house mariachi bands; a black band, a white band and a maroon band. Eventually one will come over and surround you and then you can't miss it. Surrounded by murals of famous mariachi singers from the 1950s, the cantina sits on the edge of Plaza Garibaldi in downtown Mexico City, the home of the mariachi.

They hang out on the street; they play on-demand in the square and they step out into the road to hail passing cars. They are waiting to be commissioned, to be sent off to play to someone, somewhere in this dark, sprawling city for some special occasion or maybe jump in your truck and party with you. Imagine the joy of receiving a mariachi band on your doorstep; they are there to serenade you. How would that make you feel about the music and the person who had sent it? Nobody knows what the word "mariachi" means or where it comes from. I ask several people and get different answers.

A group of local residents arrives and occupies the booth next to us. They are in for a serious night. They order a very expensive bottle of cognac, which they proceed to drink mixed with cheap cola.

They summons the white-costumed mariachi band. The lead singer wears big mustachios and a military style costume different from the players. They assemble, squeezing between seats and tables. The singers and violinist's stand right in front of the table, the contra-basso player stands with his stately massive acoustic guitar, some distance away. The two trumpet players stand even further away by the door of the cantina. It's as close as they can get, but they're loud enough, they don't need to be close like the violins.

One of the party has a birthday this evening. Each time she chooses a song for the mariachi to sing to her, she is choosing to be happy or sad. She wants them to create an emotional bond. She wants the singer to perform the tragedy of the song. She wants him to channel the pure joy. It is not a dramatic performance of varying emotion. It is a commitment of intensity to the music. It is a statement at her own table that this music is serious and real and that he will bring it into her heart. She chooses a sad song because she wants to cry. She knows that it is a performance. She knows that he is just a mariachi. She knows that he is not a character in the song; there is no role-play here. She does not enter the narrative with the mariachi. She accesses it via him. But the song is old. It is traditional. She already knows where it is going. They have all lived with this song and what it can do. They have known its power since they were babies. The whole culture grows up experiencing their most intense emotions through the shaman power of the mariachi. The songs are tokens for the stories that they tell.

She chooses the song to match the narrative she wishes to revisit. The only question is how well the mariachi can perform his role. How far can he vanish into the pure intense stream of emotion he and his fellow musicians create? I want to hear the mariachi channel the love that my lover is sending me. I do not fall in love with the mariachi but he changes my emotional state. He alters my condition by his singing. I cry, I dance, I am seduced. But the mariachi in his black or his white uniform is only the messenger. He is a worker. I recognize his role. I value it. I'll pay him to play ten songs at my table. He creates the intensification that I am here for. I would not come to this table if I do not want him to play for me. He is playing out to me a set of coded musical messages that I have understood and sought out since childhood. He is like a doctor or a lawyer. He performs a professional service with complete professionalism – most of the time. Unless by chance one of his band gets too drunk or over-affectionate, starts putting his arm round the audience. Then he breaks the spell.

There is no camaraderie with the Mariachi. An audience may recognize them as individual people, but that vanishes when they burst into song. When they launch into the music, the audience is transported too. It is not like the crowd who is idolizing the hero pop star. The music is timeless and filled with every other moment in life in which it has appeared. It is a transport into a collective experience. It is the emotional consciousness that the nation shares, but defined and personal for each individual, shaped by how they personally heard the music. It feels like nothing else. It is authentic despite the artifice of the performer. It is the vibration of the real experience that the listener holds in her heart. She does not disappear into some collective mist. It is an affirmation of her identity. She cries over the memory of her dead mother because the song gives her the permission to do so, which is what she requested.

Glossary

2400 Baud - Measure of speed of throughput of a digital signal through the analogue modem

AACR2 - Advanced Audio Coding (revision 2)

AOL - America Online

Beta release - a release that is still being tested or is in development

B2B - Business to business

B2C - Business to consumer

BPI - British Phonographic Industry - UK trade association for record companies

CD - Compact Disc

CD-ROM - Compact Disc - Read-only Memory

CISAC - Conference International Des Societees des Auteurs et Compositeurs

CODEC - coder decoder - refers to algorithmic method of compressing digital audio into small file size, such as mp3, wma, aac, ogg.

Dark Fibre - cable that has not been provisioned or limited but has theoretically full bandwidth capability

DCC - Digital Compact Cassette

DEA - Digital Economy Act

DVD - Digital Video Disc

ECD - Enhanced Compact Disc

FAC - Featured Artists Coalition

IFPI - International Federation of Phonographic Industries - Global trade association for record companies

IPO - Initial Public Offering

ISP - Internet service provider

MD - Mini Disc

Modem - A combined device for modulation and demodulation, for example, between the digital data of a computer and the analog signal of a telephone line

MMF - Music Managers Forum

MPEG - Moving Pictures Expert Group

MP3 - MPEG-2 Audio Layer III

MU - Musicians' Union

P2P - Peer to peer - particular method for distribution using individual's computing power

PPL - Phonographic Performance Limited - UK collecting society for record companies and performers responsible for collecting non-interactive broadcast and internet media royalties

PRS - Performing Rights Society - UK collecting society for publishers, composers and songwriters

RIAA - Record Industry Association of America - US trade association for record companies

SDMI - Secure Digital Music Initative

SuperJaneet - Superfast Joint Academic Network - the UK highspeed broadband network for universities

VC - Venture Capitalist

Acknowledgements

I'm grateful to a lot of people who have read, commented on and corrected drafts of this text. If there are errors remaining, I apologize they're mine. I received terrific help from Sarah Thornton, Boyd Steemson, Sara Holloway, Toni Schneider, Juliana Koranteng, Glenda Thornton, and Simon Frith. Amir Gelbard, was brilliant with the design of the cover and jacket and put up with my endless changes. I have had fantastic conversations with all sorts of people who have helped refine my thinking and distill the most important elements from the morass of detail that at times threatened to overwhelm me. Thanks to Peter Jenner, Pete Downton, Paul Sanders, Nick Appleyard, Alex Stanhope, Mark Meharry, Patrick Towell, Mandy Berry, Greg Mead, David Harvey, and Alan Moore. Warmest thanks, love and affection of course go to my fabulous mum and sisters who have supported me sometimes without realizing it during the course of writing this and last but by no means least to my two amazing kids - Otto and Cora - they are the fastest growing inspirations of all.

Printed in Great Britain
by Amazon